Mobile Prototyping with Axure 7

Quickly deploy innovative user experience designs to mobile devices for responsive prototyping using the exciting new features of Axure 7

Will Hacker

[PACKT]

PUBLISHING

BIRMINGHAM - MUMBAI

Mobile Prototyping with Axure 7

First published: November 2013

Production Reference: 1191113

Published by Packt Publishing Ltd.
Livery Place
35 Livery Street
Birmingham B3 2PB, UK.

ISBN 978-1-84969-514-5

www.packtpub.com

Cover Image by Duraid Fatouhi (duraidfatouhi@yahoo.com)

Credits

Author
Will Hacker

Reviewers
Svetlin Denkov

Matt Goddard

Marina Lin

Jan Tomáš

Larry Vance

Acquisition Editor
Owen Roberts

Commissioning Editor
Neil Alexander

Technical Editors
Novina Kewalramani

Harshad Vairat

Project Coordinator
Sageer Parkar

Proofreader
Maria Gould

Indexer
Monica Ajmera Mehta

Production Coordinator
Shantanu Zagade

Cover Work
Shantanu Zagade

About the Author

Will Hacker is a Lead Interaction Designer at GE Capital, where he works on multidevice designs for commercial lending software. He's used Axure for several years as part of his iterative design and prototyping process, and spent two and a half years working exclusively on mobile design, prototyping, and usability testing for Cars.com. He has also written about user experience and mobile design for *Smashing Magazine* and *UX Booth*, and is a frequent speaker at UX design events in Chicago. He holds a Master's degree in Human-computer Interaction from DePaul University. He tweets at @willhacker and blogs at willhacker.net.

No book is ever written by just one person. There are always people working behind the scenes to make it come together. I'd like to thank my editors, Neil Alexander and Neha Nagwekar, for proposing the idea for this book and for guiding it to completion. Thank you for your faith in me. I also want to thank Sageer Parkar for coordinating the project and keeping us all on task. Thanks also goes to my technical editors Harshad Vairat and Novina Kewalramani. Their attention to the small details was invaluable. I also want to thank my reviewers Matt Goddard and Jan Tomáš. Additional thanks goes to my friends and colleagues Svetlin Denkov, Marina Lin, and Larry Vance, who read rough draft chapters and provided feedback and encouragement throughout the project. This book would not have come together without their support and honest critique. Thanks also to Ezra Schwartz, who encouraged me to pursue the project and provided advice and inspiration along the way. And finally, a special thanks to my wife, Kathy, who offered encouragement, patience, and understanding during long nights and weekends at the keyboard. Her belief in me makes everything I do possible.

About the Reviewers

Svetlin Denkov is a UX Prototyper at GN ReSound in Chicago, where he builds highly interactive prototypes for mobile and tablet devices. He has used Axure for several years as his tool of choice for building and testing iterative prototypes. He holds a Master's degree in HCI from DePaul University. He is also a local leader for the Chicago Chapter of IxDA, which introduces technology events to the UX Chicago community monthly. He regularly contributes at the Chicago Axure Meetup, and helps others on the Axure forums as an expert user under the name `light_forger`. He tweets about UX, innovation, and technology at `@svetlindenkov` and can be reached at `www.linkedin.com/in/svetlindenkov`.

Matt Goddard has worked in the user experience / software development industry for over 15 years. Through his company, UX Media, he helps his clients to understand the demands of their products or services on their customer's life and offers them strategies for matching business and customer goals.

Marina Lin is an Interaction Designer for mobile apps at `Cars.com` where she uses Axure for prototyping Android and iOS apps. She holds a Master's degree in Information Architecture from the Illinois Institute of Technology. She recently contributed a chapter to the textbook *Negotiating Cultural Encounters: Narrating Intercultural Engineering and Technical Communication*. Her work has also appeared in *Boxes and Arrows, User Experience Magazine*, and *Business Communication Quarterly*.

Jan Tomáš found the beauty of user experience design during his studies at the Czech Technical University in Prague and Tokyo University of Agriculture and Technology. Currently, he works as a User Experience Specialist at GMC Software Technology which delivers solutions in the field of customer communications management in all over the world. His specialization deals with user research and prototyping. He uses Axure RP on a daily basis for prototyping web and mobile applications to communicate his designs with developers, managers, and other stakeholders. He is also an active member of the user experience community. He organizes meetings called UX Circus Show every month to share knowledge and to show that their jobs can be fun.

Larry Vance has been practicing UX since 1999. He's currently a Senior Interaction Designer at Cars.com, responsible for inventory search and listings. He was hooked on Axure from day one and is convinced it's well on its way to becoming "the Photoshop of Interaction Design".

www.PacktPub.com

Support files, eBooks, discount offers and more

You might want to visit www.PacktPub.com for support files and downloads related to your book.

Did you know that Packt offers eBook versions of every book published, with PDF and ePub files available? You can upgrade to the eBook version at www.PacktPub.com and as a print book customer, you are entitled to a discount on the eBook copy. Get in touch with us at service@packtpub.com for more details.

At www.PacktPub.com, you can also read a collection of free technical articles, sign up for a range of free newsletters and receive exclusive discounts and offers on Packt books and eBooks.

http://PacktLib.PacktPub.com

Do you need instant solutions to your IT questions? PacktLib is Packt's online digital book library. Here, you can access, read and search across Packt's entire library of books.

Why Subscribe?
- Fully searchable across every book published by Packt
- Copy and paste, print and bookmark content
- On demand and accessible via web browser

Free Access for Packt account holders

If you have an account with Packt at www.PacktPub.com, you can use this to access PacktLib today and view nine entirely free books. Simply use your login credentials for immediate access.

Table of Contents

Preface

Mobile app and responsive web design are some of the most important topics in software development today. One of the key aspects of high-quality user experience design is prototyping, as a means to test our ideas and see where they work and where they don't. In this book we look at one of the latest prototyping tools, Axure RP 7. This book is not meant to be an exhaustive look at the many features in Axure 7, but rather is intended to introduce experienced Axure users to some of the mobile prototyping features in the latest version of this widely-used tool.

What this book covers

Chapter 1, *Prototypes and Why We Use Them*, provides an overview of what digital prototypes are and how they are used in software design and development. This chapter will focus specifically on the role prototypes play in mobile app and website development.

Chapter 2, *Mobile Design Concepts*, introduces readers to important mobile design concepts and constraints and shows how mobile design differs from desktop application design.

Chapter 3, *Installing and Setting Up Axure*, shows readers how to get Axure RP 7 and how to set up a basic mobile design project.

Chapter 4, *Building Mobile Prototypes*, shows how to set up a basic mobile website prototype and design basic mobile interactions.

Chapter 5, *Adaptive Views*, explores the new Adaptive Views feature in Axure RP 7 that lets us prototype responsive web designs.

Chapter 6, *Mobile Interactions*, covers some of the basic interactions used in mobile website and application design so we can make our prototypes as realistic as possible.

Chapter 7, Drag-and-drop, covers basic drag-and-drop events and interactions that are common in mobile gaming and other applications.

Chapter 8, Viewing on Mobile Devices, shows how to get your prototypes on actual mobile devices for demonstration and testing.

Appendix, Axure and Mobile Design Resources, provides a list of resources for Axure prototyping and general mobile design concepts.

The *Bonus Chapter, Best Practices,* outlines some of the most effective and well accepted procedures used when working with Axure. This chapter is available at `https://www.packtpub.com/sites/default/files/downloads/5145OT_Best_Practices.pdf`.

What you need for this book

To use this book you need a Mac or Windows computer, the latest version of Axure RP 7, and mobile devices to actually view and test our designs on the device. You should also create a free AxShare account, which will allow us to host up to 10 prototypes in a cloud-based environment so we can view them anywhere on real devices.

Who this book is for

This book is for experienced Axure users who want exposure to mobile design concepts and the specific features Axure 7 offers for mobile prototyping. The goal of the book is to help us take our Axure prototyping skills to the next level and start designing and testing mobile prototypes. You should be familiar with prototyping practices and Axure specifically before reading this book.

Conventions

In this book, you will find a number of styles of text that distinguish between different kinds of information. Here are some examples of these styles, and an explanation of their meaning.

Code words in text are shown as follows: "Libraries are simply Axure RP files containing reusable components that are saved with a `.RPLIB` file extension."

New terms and **important words** are shown in bold. Words that you see on the screen, in menus or dialog boxes for example, appear in the text like this: "The name we assign to the page is what will appear for each item in the **Widgets** panel".

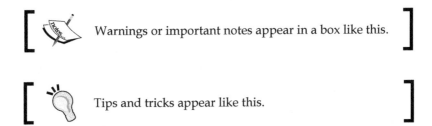

Warnings or important notes appear in a box like this.

Tips and tricks appear like this.

Reader feedback

Feedback from our readers is always welcome. Let us know what you think about this book—what you liked or may have disliked. Reader feedback is important for us to develop titles that you really get the most out of.

To send us general feedback, simply send an e-mail to feedback@packtpub.com, and mention the book title via the subject of your message.

If there is a topic that you have expertise in and you are interested in either writing or contributing to a book, see our author guide on www.packtpub.com/authors.

Customer support

Now that you are the proud owner of a Packt book, we have a number of things to help you to get the most from your purchase.

Errata

Although we have taken every care to ensure the accuracy of our content, mistakes do happen. If you find a mistake in one of our books—maybe a mistake in the text or the code—we would be grateful if you would report this to us. By doing so, you can save other readers from frustration and help us improve subsequent versions of this book. If you find any errata, please report them by visiting http://www.packtpub.com/submit-errata, selecting your book, clicking on the **errata submission form** link, and entering the details of your errata. Once your errata are verified, your submission will be accepted and the errata will be uploaded on our website, or added to any list of existing errata, under the Errata section of that title. Any existing errata can be viewed by selecting your title from http://www.packtpub.com/support.

Piracy

Piracy of copyright material on the Internet is an ongoing problem across all media. At Packt, we take the protection of our copyright and licenses very seriously. If you come across any illegal copies of our works, in any form, on the Internet, please provide us with the location address or website name immediately so that we can pursue a remedy.

Please contact us at copyright@packtpub.com with a link to the suspected pirated material.

We appreciate your help in protecting our authors, and our ability to bring you valuable content.

Questions

You can contact us at questions@packtpub.com if you are having a problem with any aspect of the book, and we will do our best to address it.

1
Prototypes and Why We Use Them

It's impossible to design the perfect product the first time we try. It's not that we are not smart designers, it's just the nature of our craft that we need to work through several versions of an idea before our creation can approach a more perfect form.

This is where prototyping comes in. Prototypes allow us to build a digital representation of a user experience that can be put on a real device and shared with users. Prototypes are essentially communication tools that allow us to share proposed functionality with users and stakeholders to see if our designs address their user goals and business needs, and collect feedback from them in return. Prototyping can help us from making expensive mistakes that can damage our companies and their reputations.

In this chapter we will take a look at the role prototypes play in software development and how we can benefit from them as user experience designers and software developers. We will look specifically at:

- The reasons for prototyping
- How Axure RP 7 fits into our work
- Deciding on a level of fidelity for our prototypes
- Situations when we may not want to create a prototype

Reasons for prototyping

We prototype so we can fail. Yes, so we can fail, but in a safe manner. While we don't usually want to fail at our work, the goal of prototyping is really to find flaws in our designs while we are still in the early phases of a design project. As we find the design problems, either in our screen flows or the user interface, we can try new design solutions before we get to the development stage. A rapid, iterative approach to design allows potential problems to shake out at the **UX** (**User Experience**) design phase, before expensive development work begins. If we skip what I call the "prototype-test-rework-repeat" phase, we can be left with design flaws that have to be fixed in the real application. This is more costly to your business and can alienate customers and stakeholders, if those design flaws made it into the final product.

But prototyping isn't new, and didn't begin with the software industry. *Michelangelo* and *Leonardo da Vinci* created hand-drawn studies of works that they would eventually render in paint or stone. Architects build scale paper and wood models of buildings to better communicate the final design and appearance to their clients. Automobile manufacturers create full-sized working prototypes of future vehicles they refer to as "concept cars" that are used to see how the public and industry react to the design of a new body style and other future features. In short, prototypes allow us to explore and interact with designs of all kinds of things before we commit them to stone, steel, or expensive application code.

The RITE way to prototype

One way I've seen prototyping work in a real-world setting is by using a method known as **RITE** (**Rapid Iterative Testing and Evaluation**). This is a method of usability testing in which we make changes to the prototype between individual sessions. The goal is to remove usability issues once they have been encountered a few times, so we can learn about other problems that we may not have seen yet because of the earlier ones. This makes our test sessions more informative by uncovering more problems than we would by testing one prototype.

I've conducted many mobile app and website usability test sessions using prototypes created completely in Axure. In one such test, as the test team learned about problems with the visibility of some of the interface elements, a team member was able to make changes to the prototype in between test sessions and the problems disappeared, allowing us to learn about new usability problems.

Working smarter with prototypes

Taking the extra steps to create and test a prototype can make us more productive in the long run. Consider this fictitious example:

Imagine a newly launched airline website where people can only select their seat after they purchase a ticket. Now imagine the cancelations and calls to support centers that follow when frequent fliers find they can no longer see and choose their seat before buying a ticket. Corporate customers are enraged because of the inconvenience to their traveling workforce and bad public relations follow. Airline management can't allow this. The ticket purchase process will have to be reengineered at a substantial cost of time and money. This only damages the airline's bottom line and leaves its customers angry.

Welcome to a world without prototypes. It is not a pretty place.

In the case of our fictitious airline website, changes will need to be made to the purchase process. These can come at a substantial cost and it may not be possible to pass these costs along to customers because airlines operate in competitive and price-sensitive markets. The airline's website project will be less successful than hoped for and could create a long-lasting negative impression of the brand among frequent fliers of the carrier.

Similar mistakes are made everyday in software development. Product managers and designers make important decisions about significant design details without feedback from the final users and risk the success of their products and potentially the future of their companies.

Jared Spool, founder of User Interface Engineering, discusses prototyping in his September 20, 2012 column, *Exploring the Problem Space Through Prototyping* at `http://www.uie.com/articles/four_phases_prototyping/`:

> *Design is all about tradeoffs. Learning how each tradeoff affects the outcome is core to great design.*
>
> *One of the things we saw from the best designers is their use of prototypes to explore the problem. The prototype is the instrument they used to uncover previously hidden constraints and to see the shifts in the outcome of the design.*

Spool concludes:

> *In the end, it's all about creating great designs. Those designs are great because they find the best intersection of the users, technology, and business dimensions. That can only happen when the team really understands the landscape of the problem space. Prototypes are an effective tool for exploring that landscape.*

This is why prototyping and iterative user research are invaluable parts of successful user experience design.

Axure RP for prototyping

This is where tools such as Axure RP come in. I've been prototyping digital user experiences with Axure for several years, and for the last two and a half years have focused heavily on mobile web prototyping with Axure. What Axure allows us to do is build interactive prototypes without knowing HTML, CSS, or any programming language.

Another advantage of Axure is that it generates HTML as its final output, so our prototypes can be tested on various smartphone operating systems. Axure allows us to get a touchable, interactive prototype on an iPhone or Android device without having to worry about Objective-C or Java code.

Fidelity decisions

Once we start prototyping, we quickly find out that we need to decide to what degree of fidelity we need to make our prototype. Fidelity refers to the degree of realism in our prototype. The level of fidelity needed will change throughout a project. In the early stages of a project, lower fidelity prototypes are acceptable to quickly iterate on ideas. As we advance our design through the project, higher levels of fidelity will better inform stakeholders what the final product will look like. It's always important to understand what the purpose of a prototype is before making decisions about fidelity so it has the appropriate level of design, but not too much. A prototype with close-to-final layouts, graphics, and color schemes is considered high fidelity. One that is more wireframe-like and less polished is considered low fidelity. There is no correct approach to take. We need to ask ourselves what questions we are trying to answer and what degree of fidelity will help us to answer them.

We usually don't want to develop our prototypes beyond the degree of fidelity we need for our purpose, because an Axure prototype will never be the start of any production code development effort. That's not to say all prototypes are throw-away works, as we may update them many times over the course of a long project; but prototyping more functionally than you need for the test or demonstration you are preparing is usually not advisable.

Fortunately, Axure allows us to prototype at any degree of fidelity we choose, and even includes a **Page Style** setting that lets us create prototypes with a sketchy effect. **Page Style** settings in Axure allow us to create prototypes with low-fidelity sketchy effects, so viewers of the prototype won't think they are looking at a finished design. The following screenshot illustrates this:

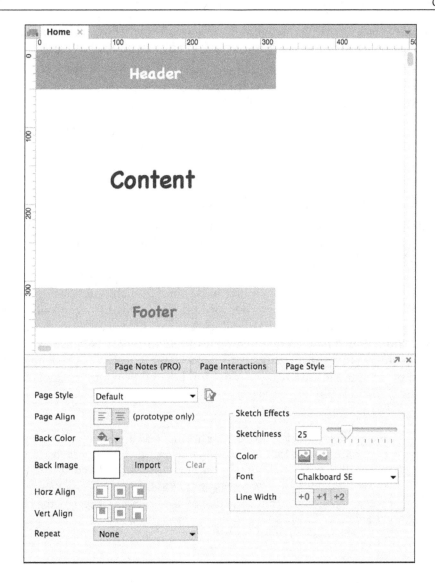

Some typical questions we need to answer at this point in the process are:

- Will we need final graphics and colors, or are placeholder images and gray scale design acceptable?

- Will we be creating a prototype that is deep or wide? That is, will our prototype address a few screen flows (or maybe just one) in great detail (a deep prototype), or are we looking at testing an overall information design and navigation scheme that doesn't need to have every possible flow built out (a wide prototype)?

- Will we be performing usability testing control labeling and nomenclature, such that a lower-fidelity boxes-and-text approach may suffice?

- Will we be testing a well-developed visual design in which we need to understand whether certain colors and controls are visible, understandable, and useable? This would call for a higher degree of fidelity.

The answers to these questions are going to determine the level of fidelity you need and should be answered before you start the actual prototyping work.

When not to prototype

There will be times when creating a prototype is not the best approach. Early in the design process, we are better served by sketching and whiteboarding our designs and screen flows. These are very lightweight design approaches that allow for rapid iteration with less time and effort lost, if you decide to change design directions. Clients and stakeholders are more willing to be open in their reactions to sketches compared to high-fidelity prototypes because they may assume after seeing an interactive prototype that the work is well under way. One sketching method is **sketchboarding**, which focuses on creating as many different sketches as possible of a design solution in a short period. This allows many design approaches to be considered by a team without designers getting bogged down in the tools used for wireframing or prototyping.

For a good introduction to sketchboarding, refer to the column by *Brandon Schauer, Sketchboards: Discover Better + Faster UX Solutions* on the *Adaptive Path* website at http://www.adaptivepath.com/ideas/ sketchboards-discover-better-faster-ux-solutions.

If you are new to sketching as a part of user experience design, the book *Sketching User Experiences: Getting the Design Right and the Right Design* by *Bill Buxton* is a good place to start.

Axure Version 7

In early July 2013, the first beta version of Axure RP 7 was released with enhanced support for mobile prototyping. The most notable new feature for mobile designers is **Adaptive Views**. Adaptive Views is Axure's implementation of support for responsive design. Responsive design is an approach to web development in which the same HTML and CSS can be delivered to smartphones, tablets, or laptops and desktops, and the device will render the content in a manner appropriate for it, usually using screen width to determine how the content should be presented. If you are familiar with HTML and CSS, you are probably familiar with responsive design. If this is a new concept to you, there are a lot of resources available online.

A great place to start learning about responsive design is by reading the seminal article about the topic, the *A List Apart* article by *Ethan Marcotte* at `http://alistapart.com/article/responsive-web-design`.

Axure 7 includes several other features to support mobile prototyping, which we will explore throughout this book.

Summary

Prototyping is the activity that can keep us from building the wrong product by allowing us to test our designs with real end users early in the design process and in an iterative manner. Because Axure doesn't require coding skills, UX designers and information architects can quickly create interactive, touchable mobile prototypes that can be tested on real devices without having to engage the development team. Prototypes also serve as a way to share designs with stakeholders early in the design process to give them a better feel for what it is we are proposing. And with its ability to get our designs on real mobile devices, Axure allows mobile designers to validate our work early in the software development process by allowing people to touch and interact with our ideas.

2
Mobile Design Concepts

So you're thinking about taking an existing design mobile or building something new exclusively for the mobile context? This chapter will give you a basic overview of designing for mobile devices. If mobile design is new to you, get ready to learn a new way of thinking about interaction and visual design. Mobile design is a good deal more complicated than designing for the desktop environment because we have to take into account usage context, unpredictable network connections, and direct manipulation of the interface in imprecise ways, such as touch and voice.

In this chapter we will take a look at some of the underlying principles of mobile design, including:

- Sketching before prototyping
- The importance of the mobile context
- Knowing our users
- Knowing our platforms
- Content as navigation
- Designing for touch
- Working with small screens
- Location and other alternative forms of input
- Mobile-friendly forms

The pencil is your first design tool

Before we get into the nuts and bolts of mobile design considerations, we need to recognize that every mobile project—smartphone or tablet, Android or Apple—should start with sketching. Our content could be displayed on a variety of devices, from smaller smartphones to larger tablets. And people may hold those devices in either portrait or landscape orientation. So we need to think through the content and how it will display in each context before starting to prototype. If we are working on a responsive web design that is targeted to smartphones, tablets, and desktop computers, we definitely need to sketch out the different ways that the content will be presented before we spend too much time in Axure (or Photoshop, or any wireframing tool). The overhead any design tool introduces gets in the way of our solving the design problem, which should always be our primary concern.

Context is king

One of the most important things to know about mobile design is to always think about the context of use. Yes, mobile operating systems and smaller screen sizes are extremely important design considerations, which we will explore as well, but context of use should serve as a guiding principle for our work.

That's because context is so important to how any mobile app or website is experienced. In desktop application development, many designers assume users will likely be sitting at a desk, table, or retail checkout counter using a laptop or desktop computer (although this is definitely not always the case). But in mobile design, we just don't know where users will be using our creations. They may be sitting at a desk, standing in a line at a hotel, sitting in the back seat of a car, walking down the street, or just stretching out on their sofa and using their mobile device because they don't want to walk to their computer to do something. This introduces a few problems for us as designers. First we have to understand why they are using our app or mobile website, and we have to have an idea of where they might be using it. This intersection of what we think we know about "the why" and "the where" is what will serve as a framework for how we approach our designs, but we just won't know the use context in many cases.

Users may be using our app outdoors on a sunny day in a ballpark. This will affect their ability to read text on backlit displays, and should cause us to think about reducing the amount of text the users need to read, and the size of the text labels on interface elements in our app. They may be using our app in crowded elevators or busy airport terminals with people occasionally bumping into them. If this is the case, we may want to make the size of our interface elements larger and may want to include ways to undo critical actions in our app. They may be using our app in a moving mass transit car, a situation where it is sometimes harder to tap small targets with precision than when a person is sitting in a stationary chair. Or they may be using it in a noisy mall, where auditory feedback might be missed. If this is a possible use case for your app, consider using the phone-vibrate mechanism to attract their attention. In any app that signals something to users with sound or visual cues, we should find a secondary way to signal these state changes.

Knowing our users

We can't really design effective and usable solutions unless we know our users. In the absence of this knowledge, all we are doing is making software based on how we think it will be used. There's a big difference, especially when we are designing for mobile. We can get ourselves into real trouble if we sit in our offices and try to rationalize how we think people use the things we make. We have to be in the field, watching people use the software, seeing how they experience it on specific devices and in specific settings, and finding out what they are hoping to accomplish if we are going to design truly great mobile experiences.

Field research is important to any kind of human interaction design, be it for software, hardware, or the physical checkout line in a department store. But field research is especially important in mobile design because people can and do take their devices anywhere and everywhere.

 For an insightful look at the value of usability testing, refer to the blog post, *If you want users to love your designs, fall in love with your users*, by *Dana Chisnell* at http://usabilitytesting.wordpress. com/2013/08/01/just-follow-the-script-working-with-pro-and-proto-pro-co-researchers/.

Fortunately, Axure 7 makes it easy for us to get our designs onto real devices, as we'll see in *Chapter 8, Viewing on Mobile Devices*.

Know the platform

It's not enough to just know what functionality our target users want. We also need to know on what platforms they will be using our creations. This topic is of importance beyond Axure design, but influences some of the choices we'll make such as which widget libraries to use. Smartphone and tablet operating system creators have published user interface guidelines. These guidelines cover the interaction paradigms and design standards employed by:

- Apple's iOS for iPhone, iPad, and iPod Touch
- Google's Android for smartphones and tablets
- Microsoft's Windows phone 7 and 8, and Windows 8 for the Surface tablet
- BlackBerry smartphones

These guidelines recommend what interaction patterns should be used in certain situations, how native interface controls should be used, and how they should behave when people interact with them. In *Appendix*, *Axure and Mobile Design Resources*, you'll find information about the interface design guidelines for the four largest mobile OS developers.

What platform to target

This is not an easy question to answer. It will depend on the needs of our company or client, or how much market penetration we want our app to have. Google's Android has the greatest distribution in raw numbers, but is spread across hundreds of devices and manufacturers, which increases the complexity of design. Apple's iOS has a much smaller footprint than Android, but because it only runs on a small set of Apple-made devices, it is often easier to design and build iOS apps. Axure prototyping is impacted by platform choice when the targeted platform makes a major change. The recent release of Apple's iOS 7, for example, means we need to create or find new widget libraries to design for it. There really is no correct answer to this question. Welcome to the often ambiguous world of mobile design.

Platform distribution

Research firm **IDC (International Data Corporation)** reported in August 2013 that Android accounted for 79.3 percent of the smartphones shipped worldwide in the second quarter of 2013, while iOS accounted for 13.2 percent (the iPhone is still the bestselling individual device, but Android's numbers are greater because it comes on hundreds of devices). Microsoft came in a distant third at 3.7 percent followed by BlackBerry at 2.9 percent. No other maker of a mobile operating system accounted for more than 1 percent of the units shipped in this period.

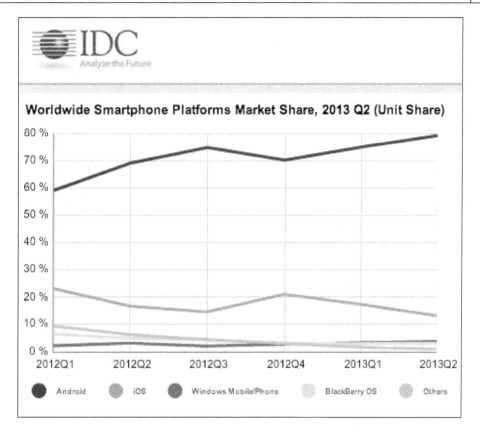

And don't forget that there is not just one version of these operating systems in the market. There are variations to each one, adding to our challenge as designers.

Apple made significant changes to the visual design of iOS when it released iOS 7. This was the first post-Steve Jobs version of iOS. The passion for simple, clear design of Apple Senior Vice President of Design *Jonathan Ive*, saw iOS completely rethought using what's known as **flat design** and moving away from the skeuomorphism that was a signature of previous versions of iOS.

While the debate between skeuomorphism versus flat design is important to designers, the main thing to know when creating prototypes in Axure is that each platform has its own visual design guidelines and language. This is what we need to be most concerned about when designing mobile prototypes.

[

Skeuomorphism versus flat design was one of the most hotly debated design topics of 2013. There is no correct answer as to which is better. There are examples of both approaches being used to produce applications with good and poor usability. We provide greater service to our users when we focus on creating usable designs, whether flat or skeuomorphic.
]

There were also changes to some iOS 7 interactions. We must be aware of these changes because our native apps are going to have to function the way users expect them to, based on the version of iOS they are using, and other apps they use that were written for it. And because we can't assume someone using iOS 7 has ever owned an Apple device running iOS 6, we can't assume they'll be familiar with interaction patterns from earlier versions of the platform.

Things get even more complicated with Android. According to the Android Developers website, at little more than 35 percent of Android phones were using some version of Android 2.x in August 2013, while more than 60 percent were using some version of Android 4.x.

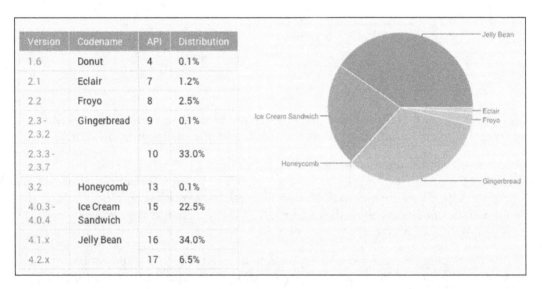

Version	Codename	API	Distribution
1.6	Donut	4	0.1%
2.1	Eclair	7	1.2%
2.2	Froyo	8	2.5%
2.3 - 2.3.2	Gingerbread	9	0.1%
2.3.3 - 2.3.7		10	33.0%
3.2	Honeycomb	13	0.1%
4.0.3 - 4.0.4	Ice Cream Sandwich	15	22.5%
4.1.x	Jelly Bean	16	34.0%
4.2.x		17	6.5%

Because there were some significant differences in interactions between Android 2.x and 4.x, we will need to know more about which version of the platform we are targeting for native app development. Designing for Android introduces additional complexity because each hardware manufacturer or cellular carrier can customize the open source OS. By comparison, iOS only runs on hardware made by Apple and does not support customization.

The network is (mostly) always available

One constraint we have to deal with as designers of mobile user experiences is cellular and data networks that are beyond our control. This means someone can be joyfully perusing our mobile website on the train or at home, only to hit a network dead zone and lose access to the next page in a flow. In native app development, we can use caching techniques to download data during the first user visit to compensate for some of this network loss. Native apps also have the advantage of having the entire GUI downloaded to the device as part of the install process.

For the mobile web, there are ways to take advantage of local storage on the device that can reduce some of the latency caused by the back-and-forth request-response nature of the Internet. We should be talking with our engineers and architects regularly to see what techniques we can employ to reduce the pain of dropped or overloaded network connections.

While this doesn't impact Axure design in a big way, we may want to conduct a usability test for how people respond to delays in our apps. We can use the **Wait** action in **Case Editor**, which is introduced later, to simulate a delayed response to a user's action.

Content is navigation

Another key consideration in designing for mobile devices is to think of content as a navigation element in itself, not something to be merely navigated through. A practical application of this is commonly seen in photo galleries, in which people can use swipe gestures to move through photo sets instead of tapping previous and next buttons. The main tenet of content as navigation is "more content, less chrome". This is necessary because mobile screen sizes are limited, so we should try to fill as much of them as possible with meaningful content and let people use gestures to explore it. As designers, we must be aware of what gestures are prevalent and what users expect from their specific mobile platform, and design affordances into our prototypes. It's not enough to design the content as navigation if that isn't apparent to users. Good examples of using content as navigation are found in Flipboard and mobile Twitter. In Flipboard, you swipe left and right to navigate through the pages of your feed and tap the content itself to drill into the full article or post. Using Twitter on a smartphone involves scrolling up and down through the feed and pulling down the entire screen to refresh the content. The only buttons, or chrome, on mobile Twitter are used to trigger off-canvas menus to display or to switch users into a new application state. To consume the main feed, no chrome is needed. The more we reduce mobile experiences to people's fingers and their interaction with content, the more engaging and less burdensome those experiences become.

Twitter's mobile app makes minimal use of chrome. Most of the user interaction is by using gestures with the content itself.

Axure's **Dynamic Panels** and drag-and-drop interactions can help simulate this kind of user experience, as we'll see in later chapters.

Designing for touch

We can't discuss designing content as navigation without recognizing touch as the main source of interaction with our mobile devices. Prior to the iPhone, mobile devices were cellular phones that sometimes could access some limited (and crippled) form of the web and were mostly designed to make calls. The hard key interfaces of what are now known as "feature phones" made it difficult to navigate through most web experiences. Unless you were making a call or setting a new ringtone, most device operations were difficult (if not impossible) to accomplish.

But that all changed in 2007 when Apple introduced the iPhone. Suddenly people had an entire screen of glass on which they could use gestures to interact with content, play games, send e-mails, update social media, send text messages, and occasionally make a phone call or two. Handheld computing had finally made the leap from indirect manipulation to direct manipulation of the interface.

Direct manipulation refers to the ability of a user to directly alter their computing environment through touch, voice, or eye movement. Indirect manipulation refers to using an intermediary device, such as a computer mouse or stylus, to affect changes in applications.

Now, the iPhone wasn't the first device to use touch as an input. Anyone who has shopped at a grocery store or gone to an airport in the last 10 years has used or seen people using touch screen devices and kiosks to interact with software. But the watershed moment of the first iPhone was that it put touch interfaces into people's hands on a device that was extremely personal and could be used on a daily basis. While the touchscreen kiosk at the airport was encountered occasionally by most people (or more often by business travelers), the touchscreen smartphone introduced people to touch interfaces and gestures on a device they would use every day. People were introduced on a mass scale to the world of touchable computing.

For a more detailed look at how touchscreens actually work and why physical measurements should be used instead of digital measurements such as pixels, refer to the excellent article *Common Misconceptions About Touch* on *UXmatters* by *Steven Hoober* at
`http://www.uxmatters.com/mt/archives/2013/03/common-misconceptions-about-touch.php`.

Touch targets

It's not enough to make touch-sensitive screens and put them on smartphones and tablets. Our designs need to fit with the platform standards people expect. Our interfaces need to be usable, and that's where the interface guidelines we discussed earlier come into play. Most OS creators provide guidelines for touch targets, which are the parts of our interface that users are supposed to interact with. The guidelines suggest a range between 7 and 10 mm, although I prefer to stick to the higher end of that range. It's best to design for the human finger and your actual users and not blindly follow the interface guidelines of the particular OS you are working on. This is where usability testing plays an important role in validating our designs.

There are also cases where we will want to make a touch target larger than the guidelines recommend. These include when making a mistake will greatly create inconvenience to the person using the app, when the person using the app has difficulty with motor control, or when the app or website will be used in lighting conditions that make the screen harder to see. In some cases, our app may be used under more than one of these conditions.

Another reason to design for the physical size of touch targets is the many differences in screen resolution and pixel density, which we will look at next.

Screen real estate

Mobile devices come in a wide variety of sizes. Just looking at two smartphones, the screens on these devices can range from the 3.5-inch screen of the iPhone 4S to the 5-inch display of the Samsung Galaxy S4 (and that's just looking at two of the most popular devices from the hundreds that are available in the market). Older BlackBerry devices with touchscreens have even less screen real estate to work with.

 Although BlackBerry use has been in steady decline for several years, we may need to work with companies or clients, such as government agencies or large financial institutions that prefer the security of BlackBerry's private network. These are cases when knowing our end users and the target platform are essential to our design and prototyping work.

Pixel density, the number of pixels available per square inch of physical screen, can also vary greatly. The Samsung S4 has a pixel density of 441 pixels per inch with a screen resolution of 1920 x 1080 pixels. The iPhone 4, 4S, and 5 all have pixel densities of 326 pixels per inch in their Retina displays, although the iPhone 5 has a larger resolution of 1136 x 640 pixels because its display is 4 inches (measured diagonally). The older iPhones are 960 x 640 pixels. These differences in screen resolution and pixel density are why you want to focus on physical size when designing interface elements. No matter what the size or specifications of the device are, the person using the device is still using it with human fingers.

Another factor to consider when designing for mobile devices is whether the app or website will be used predominantly with the person's thumb or fingers. Thumbs are larger so knowing this will aid us in making design choices.

What all these differences mean for us when we are building our prototypes in Axure is that we need to know as much as we can about the devices and the people we are targeting. If we control the device for which we are building the prototype, we can better ensure that it will fit the screen correctly.

Screen size also influences mobile design because we have less screen size to work with than when designing for desktops or laptops, especially when designing for smartphones. So our designs need to be more focused, use less text in labels, and be easier for people to understand at a glance. That at-a-glance ease of use is especially important when the app or website will be used in one of the challenging contexts discussed earlier.

Working with gestures

Another aspect of designing for mobile and touchscreens is consideration of the gestures available on the platform we are targeting. Smartphones now support multitouch gestures (gestures that use more than one finger) so the number of gestures available to us as designers has grown since the release of that first iPhone. Some developers have also written their own gestures into apps, which can present usability challenges if people are not expecting these gestures to exist.

Another design challenge with gestures is making them visible or at least intuitive for people to discover. By their nature, gestures are not displayed on the screen, so some affordance is needed to cue the user that there may be a gesture they can use. One commonly-used technique seen in photo galleries or other interfaces is to show a small bit of the next piece of content that is mostly off screen. A little bit of animation, like the slight movement of an object on the screen, can provide visual guidance to the user about how the navigation works. These affordances and animations provide visual cues to the user that they can slide the list of content elements either left and right or up and down.

A good rule of thumb when designing for touch interfaces is to see if there is a gesture that is native to the platform that will work for your app or website. Native gestures have a better chance of being understood by people because they will be used in other apps and for functionality within the OS itself.

One way of mitigating the risk of your app failing in the market when multitouch gestures are used is to conduct frequent usability tests to see if the gesture is visible, expected, and memorable. Axure 7 can trigger interactions after detecting some gestures, a topic we will explore further in *Chapter 6, Mobile Interactions*, when we look at prototyping mobile interactions.

Alternative inputs

The variety of input mechanisms available to mobile devices is one of the things that makes designing for mobile both challenging and a lot of fun. While desktops and laptops are limited to the keyboard, mouse, and more often now, touch, mobile devices have a variety of sensors that can be employed to create engaging experiences.

Location

With location awareness now built into mobile devices, we can design apps that can find restaurants or stores for people without them having to enter a physical location on a virtual keyboard. If our apps and websites need location information for any function, we can now get that information with minimal user effort (they may have to grant us access to location information with a single tap, depending on the app or platform in question).

Yelp, for example, lets us find restaurants that are near our current location.

Compass

Many smartphones now have compasses built into them. This opens the door to some very creative designs because we can potentially know where a person is standing and in what direction they are looking. Clever app makers have used these two inputs to create walking tours of historic cities, among other uses. Belgian beer maker **Stella Artois** created an augmented reality app, **Le Bar Guide**, that a person could hold up to see restaurants and bars in the direction they were facing that served Stella's beer. That app lets people review the place they were at and invite friends who were nearby to join them. It's creative uses of device capabilities like this that make thinking about inputs in mobile an entirely fresh way of thinking about design and technology.

Accelerometer

Accelerometers can detect the movement and angle of a mobile device. We as designers can use this to alter the screen display of our apps as the user alters the device orientation between portrait and landscape views. But this also requires that we consider both orientations in our design.

How much we alter the display based on device orientation depends on the app or website we are working on. For a simple news website that presents lists of articles that link to full articles, changes in design based on device orientation change can be as simple as making the lists and articles wider or narrower. But in a more complicated application, such as a financial calculator, some functions can be hidden behind a menu in portrait orientation but displayed on the default view screen in landscape orientation (Apple does this with the calculator in iOS 7).

The **Calculator** app in iOS 7 for the iPhone uses the accelerometer to alter its display and functionality when the user changes device orientation. In portrait view, it is a standard calculator, while in landscape view it becomes a scientific calculator.

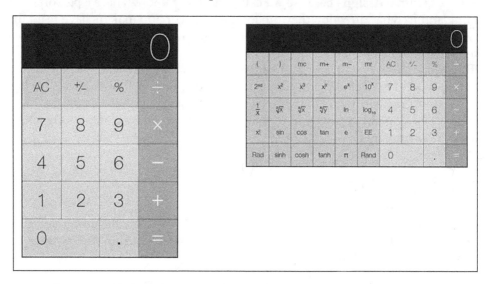

We'll see in *Chapter 5*, *Adaptive Views* that Axure 7 has added the Adaptive Views feature that allows us to design landscape and portrait views of our apps and toggle between the views based on device orientation.

Another novel use for the accelerometer is using a shake of the phone to trigger some functionality. The popular restaurant search app from **Urbanspoon** uses a shaking motion to randomly select a neighborhood near your location and a type of restaurant if you can't decide where you want to eat, or just to explore something new.

The accelerometer has also been used for many augmented reality apps, games, and utilities, such as a digital carpenter's spirit level. When **Google Maps** detects a user shaking their phone, it assumes the user is frustrated and offers a chance to provide feedback.

Camera

The camera built into modern smartphones can take high resolution photos that can be used as search inputs with services, such as **Google Goggles**.

Voice

Voice Search by Google and **Siri** by Apple have introduced mobile users to speech as an input to a computing environment. Being able to speak a search without using the keyboard is a great advantage for people who don't like or have difficulty using the virtual keyboards on smartphones.

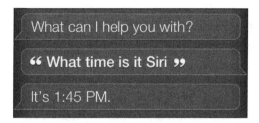

Barcodes and QR codes

The ability to scan barcodes and QR codes has changed the way people can acquire information on their mobile devices, especially smartphones. Both barcodes and **QR (Quick Response)** codes use graphic representations to store data that can be read by machine through the process of scanning. QR codes can represent a greater amount of data and have gotten a lot of attention in 2013 as marketers used them on products, at tradeshows, and in other places to allow people to capture URLs, business card information, or other data with a simple scan using their device camera. Originally invented for the automotive industry to track vehicle parts, QR codes have become another of many novel ways to input data into a mobile device.

A barcode to the left-hand side with a QR code to the right-hand side is shown in the following screenshot:

As we've already seen, there are a lot of novel ways to input data into a mobile device that have nothing to do with the forms and controls we are familiar with from the desktop web and none of which involved using a virtual keyboard. But since the Web is made up of a lot of forms, many of which are critical to getting our business done, we should look at a few design guidelines for creating mobile-friendly forms.

Mobile-friendly forms

I think *Luke Wroblewski* said it best in his book *Web Form Design: Filling in the Blanks*, "Forms Suck". At the time he wrote those two words, he was referring to the website forms we all deal with on desktops and laptops. As bad as forms can be on the desktop, they are an order of magnitude worse on a mobile device with a virtual keyboard. This section should help us build forms that are at least not as onerous a burden for our users.

Serve up the right keyboard

This design guideline is drop-dead simple. If you are asking people to provide a certain piece of information, make sure you give them a keyboard that makes it as easy as possible for them do so. Typing on a mobile device is hard enough, so don't make it worse by making people switch between keyboards. Anyone who's worked in e-commerce knows that there is significant drop-off at each stage of the checkout or enrollment process, so why not mitigate some of this risk by reducing form friction for our users.

Thankfully most mobile devices allow us to serve up keyboards that are designed to capture the data we are after. If you want an e-mail address, you can present a text input and keyboard that is tailored for that use and has all the keys a user needs to provide the information that we want.

If we are designing for the mobile web and using HTML5, there are several types of keyboards we can serve up, which are determined by the `type` attribute of the `input` tag. For example:

- `<input type="email" />`: This triggers a keyboard with the @ symbol and a period
- `<input type="number" />`: This triggers a keyboard with numeric digits plus characters, such as the dollar sign, comma, and period (when the device's language setting is English)
- `<input type="tel" />`: This triggers a keyboard with a 10-digit keypad for dialing phone numbers

- `<input type="search" />`: This triggers a keyboard with a **Search** button and in iOS will present the text input with the same rounded corners as the **Spotlight** search for iOS

- `<input type="url" />`: This triggers a keyboard with the characters needed to type a URL, including a **.com** button on iOS and some Android devices

These same types of inputs can also be invoked from native Android and iOS apps, so there is no reason our users should have to switch back-and-forth between keyboard modes to supply us with a simple piece of information.

Axure 7 added support for mobile input types in its **Widget Properties and Style** dialog box. Now, we can make our prototypes look a little closer to the final user experience we would create, removing another distraction for users in our usability tests. In the following screenshot, we see all the form types that are supported in Axure 7. We'll see another example of this in *Chapter 6, Mobile Interactions*, when we look at prototyping mobile interactions.

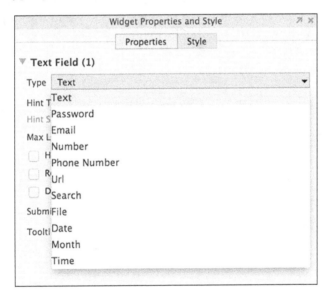

Making the field fit the finger

Another bit of advice I would offer on mobile form design is to make form fields finger friendly. In designing our form fields, we should follow the same guidelines we would for touch targets because form interactions for mobile users are often a sequence of touch, type, tap, advance, and repeat.

```
http://gizmodo.com/5431120/stella-artois-uses-augmented-reality-in-
cool-iphone-app
```

Summary

As we've seen, there is lot to consider and think about when designing for mobile devices. We have constraints brought by the ever-changing mobile usage context as well as advantages brought by device capabilities that give us access to information not available in desktop computing.

We are working with a very personal form of computing. People have their phones with them often from the time they wake up until they go to sleep. And when they sleep, many have their phones only a few inches away. This offers us the ability to create highly personalized user experiences that can take into account where the user is, what kinds of media might be on their device, and how they may want to use it.

Our users are now armed with cameras, barcode scanners, voice recorders, GPS mapping systems, and an ever-increasing amount of processor power that makes advanced computing possible. But they also live in a world of ambient distractions, slow or dropped network connections, and information overload. It is our job as designers to create experiences that add richness and value in this context, because if we fail to do so, our app may be the next one they delete.

3

Installing and Setting Up Axure

Getting up and running with Axure RP 7 is pretty easy. Once the software is installed you'll be able to check for updates to stay in sync with the latest bug fixes and enhancements. And if you're an Axure 6.5 user, the upgrade to Version 7 is free. So let's get started.

Installing Axure

The first thing you need to do is get Axure installed on your computer. Axure can be installed on Mac and Windows computers, and files can be shared between the two platforms. Go to http://www.axure.com/download and download the 30-day free trial. If you are a Version 6.5 user, you'll just need to enter your licensee name and license key and you'll be ready to use the software. If you are new to Axure, you'll receive your license key after you make your payment. Licenses are managed from the **Manage License Key...** option of the **Help** menu. Axure is licensed to one user for two computers. This allows a single user to run a licensed copy on a Mac and a PC, or on a desktop computer and a laptop.

When purchasing Axure, you will need to decide if you want to get the Standard or Pro edition. The Pro edition has all the features of the Standard edition, plus extra features for generating specifications documents, and using Axure in a shared project environment. If you are working with a team where multiple members are working on the same prototype, shared project features, such as versioning and page check in and check out, can be invaluable. To see a comprehensive comparison of the two editions, visit http://www.axure.com/compare. The Standard edition costs $289 and the Pro edition costs $589.

Files saved in Axure 7 cannot be opened in earlier versions. Create a backup copy of any RP file saved with an older version, if you think you may need to use that software version to edit it again.

Setting things up

Once you have the software installed, the next thing you'll want to do is get the workspace set up in a way that works for you. Axure has several panels in its workspace that you will use on a regular basis as you build your prototypes. The following screenshot is the default view you'll see the first time when you create a new project in Axure 7. You can customize this setup as seen in the following screenshot to make the environment work the way that's best for you:

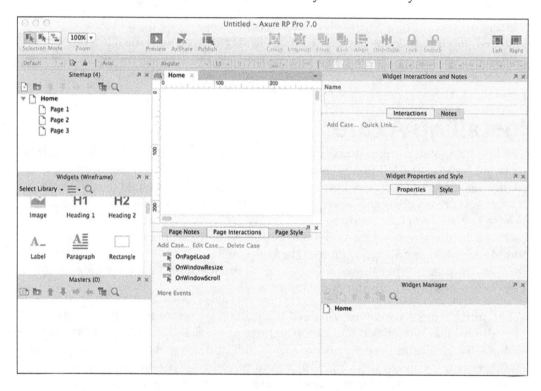

The workspace

The Axure 7 workspace is organized into several areas. The **Sitemap** panel is also where check in / check out of pages is done on shared projects.

Sitemap

The **Sitemap** panel is where all of the pages of a prototype are listed. For large prototypes, I often create empty pages at the first level of the hierarchy to represent logical groups of pages, and then place all the working pages under them as child pages. This helps me organize larger projects. One example of this type of organization might be an e-commerce prototype where we may have groups of pages for areas of the site, such as search, category browsing, and checkout. Organizing our pages this way makes it easier to find them and is helpful when new team members are joining larger projects.

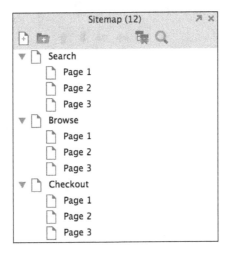

Widgets

The **Widgets (Wireframe)** panel is where the libraries of objects we can use in a prototype are available. Axure 7 comes with two widget libraries installed, **Wireframe** and **Flow**. The **Wireframe** library contains common types of web page content and user interface controls for forms and navigation. The **Flow** library contains objects used to create process and task flow diagrams. Using the **Flow** library of Axure has an advantage over other flow charting tools because our process flow diagrams can be in the same RP file as the main prototype. This makes it easier to have all the requirements in one place when doing project reviews with stakeholders. And because all Axure projects generate their contents as HTML pages, reviewers only need a web browser to view our work.

Masters

Masters, which are components that can be used on every page of a prototype and updated from a single component, have an important role in mobile prototyping. I often create iOS tab bars and Android app menus using **Masters**, as well as headers and footers on mobile web designs (as seen in the following screenshot). The **Masters** panel is also where check in / check out of Masters is done on shared projects.

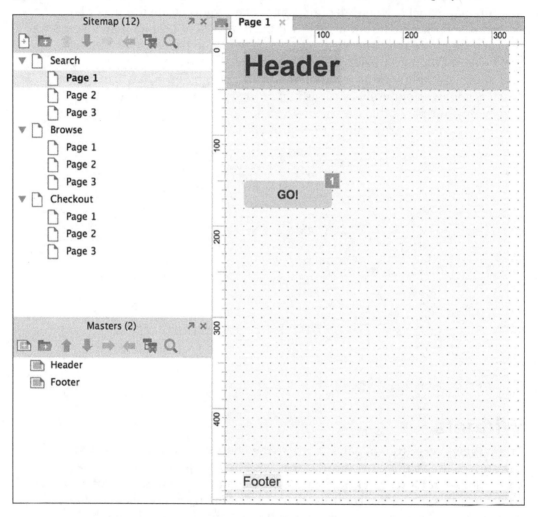

Widget Interactions and Notes

This panel is where we will create prototype interactions based on built-in Axure events that trigger responses from the prototype. If we are using Axure to build a highly interactive mobile prototype, this may be the most important panel of the workspace. Different interactions and events are available to different widgets in Axure. Buttons have **OnClick** (tap in mobile) events while **Dynamic Panels** have mobile-specific gesture events, such as **OnSwipeLeft** and **OnSwipeRight**. If you are new to Axure, spend some time learning how the events work because this is where rich, interactive prototypes really get their power. Users of the previous version of Axure will be pleased to find that many new events have been added. Some of Axure's events that can be detected by **Dynamic Panels** are listed in the **Widget Interactions and Notes** panel. A full list of events is revealed when the **More Events** link is clicked on.

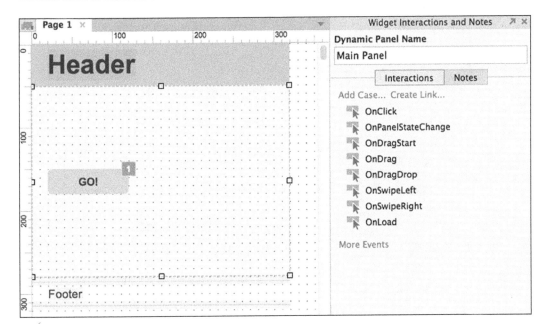

Events that I use regularly in mobile projects include **OnSwipeRight**, **OnSwipeLeft**, **OnSwipeUp**, **OnSwipeDown**, **OnLongClick**, and the drag-related events **OnDrag**, **OnDragStart**, and **OnDragStop**. For more on building interactions with events, visit http://www.axure.com/learn/basic/interactions.

This panel is also where we can add annotations much as we would in a traditional flat wireframe. **Notes** you add in Axure will display in the prototype in a web browser and are indicated by a small icon on the screen that opens the note when clicked on. **Notes** are also used when generating a specifications document. I use the **Dynamic Panel Name** and **Shape Name** fields at the top of the panel (with the text `Main Panel` in the preceding screenshot and `Go Button` in the following screenshot) to give each object a unique and understandable name. This makes it easier to find widgets later when building interactions.

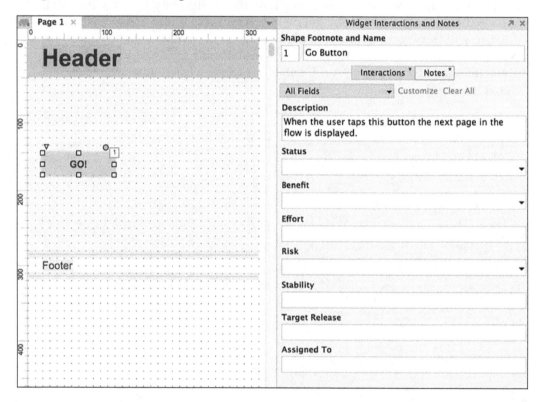

Widget Properties and Style

The managing of properties and styles for our on-screen widgets changed in Axure 7 with the introduction of the **Widget Properties and Style** panel. This panel is where we can control the shape, size, color, font, and many other attributes of a widget. It is much improved from the **Widget Style Editor** in the previous version of Axure.

While a full exploration of this new panel is beyond the scope of this book, I strongly advise you to explore it and visit the Axure forums to learn more about how it is used at http://www.axure.com/forum.

Widget Manager

The **Widget Manager** is where we can see all the widgets available to us on a screen or panel. It's also where we'll create the various states that we want in our **Dynamic Panels**, which are an important part of panel-centric design as discussed in *Chapter 4, Building Mobile Prototypes*.

One final thing to know is that we can use the **Left** and **Right** button in the main tool bar to hide or display either the left or right column. We can also close individual panels using the close icon in the top-right corner of each panel.

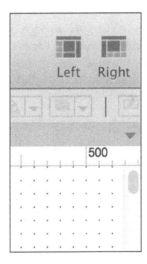

Page properties

The page properties panel is used to enter descriptive information about the page that goes into the specifications document we can generate with Axure (specifications are not within the scope of this book). We can also set page level-styles and create page interactions, such as events that can be trigged by the **OnPageLoad** event, in the page properties panel.

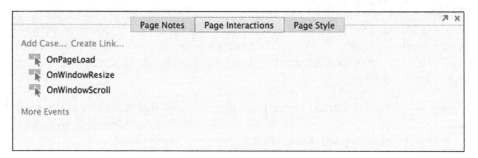

So this is the overall layout of the Axure workspace. In the following screenshot, we have a sample site structure in the **Sitemap**, **Widgets (Wireframe)** at ready access, a few simple **Masters** that can be used across our prototype, a button shape with a simple **OnClick** interaction that has also been styled to be gray with bold text, and a single **Dynamic Panel** in the **Widget Manager**.

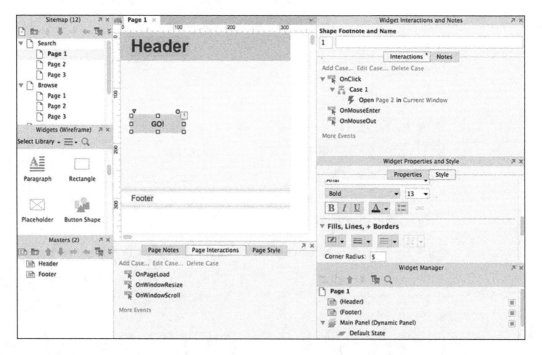

When I set up my own environment I usually close some of the panels. Once I have added all the **Masters** to my pages, I close that panel so there is more room for the **Widgets** panel to display all the individual objects I can use. I also usually close the page properties panel because I always create mobile prototypes as single-page that holds a **Dynamic Panel** with multiple states (or what I call panel-centric) prototypes. We'll look at a detailed explanation of what this means in *Chapter 4, Building Mobile Prototypes*.

Widget libraries

Now that we've looked at the main Axure workspace, let's take a look at widget libraries. Libraries are a powerful feature of Axure that allow us to create reusable components that can be used in any prototype or shared with other people. We already saw that Axure comes with the **Wireframe** and **Flow** libraries. We can also add widget libraries created by other people to our Axure environment.

Libraries are simply Axure RP files containing reusable components that are saved with a .RPLIB file extension. To create a widget library of our own, we just create a .RP file that uses each page to hold a single button, form elements, or any other type of widget. The name we assign to the page is what will appear for each item in the **Widgets** panel.

For shared projects or in corporate or agency environments where we are working with a consistent set of brand and UI elements, libraries allow us to centralize the management of those assets. And because Axure loads libraries each time it launches, changes made to the library can be distributed from a central location such as a shared network drive to save us the time and hassle of emailing a .RPLIB file to everyone on the team whenever there is a change. A project does not have to be set up as a shared project to use shared libraries as long as everyone on the team has access to the network drive where it is kept.

Axure provides access to a large set of libraries on its website and more are available from other online sources, such as the Axureland website. We can also create own libraries and share them with the larger user community through the Axure Forums.

 Axure's widget libraries are available at http://www.axure.com/download-widget-libraries. The Axureland libraries are at http://axureland.com.

To load widget libraries, select the **Load Library...** option from the menu at the right-hand side of the **Select Library** menu. The following dialog box will allow us to load a library from any drive accessible by the computer, including shared network drives. If I know I'm going to use a non-standard widget library, I will load it at the start of the project so it's available in the **Select Library** menu every time I open the project. Loaded libraries and any changes we make to the workspace are preserved, so that we can use these libraries when we reopen the project or when we create a new one. Learning to use these features can make our work much more efficient.

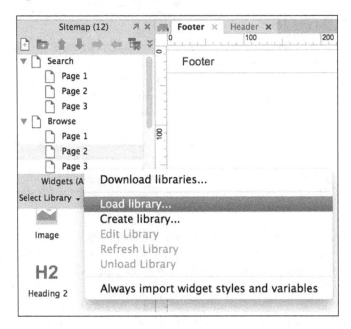

Grids

A final part of getting mobile prototyping up and running on Axure is getting our grid system set up. Grids are used in layouts that range from traditional print design to digital design as a way to provide visual order, hierarchy, and consistency to the organization of content. Grids help our designs look visually balanced and pleasing to the eye, and therefore more professional. In the following screenshot, we can see how the same page makes it easier to align the header and footer on when a grid system is in place:

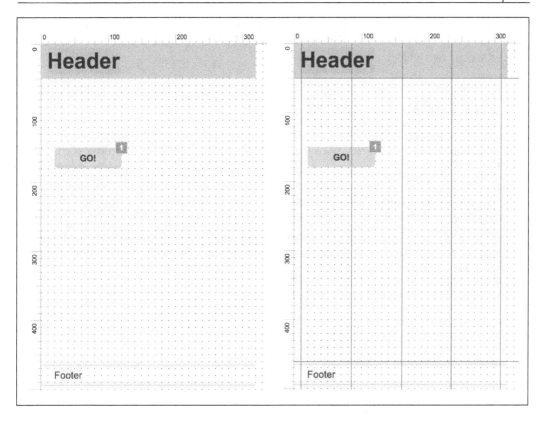

Axure's default settings are to use a 10-pixel grid using gray dots to mark the intersection of grid lines. We can use Axure's grid settings to choose lines or intersection points, grid color, and grid spacing, among other settings. You can access grid settings by choosing **Grid Settings...** from the **Grids and Guides** option of the **Arrange** menu. The submenu of the **Grids and Guides** option also provides easy access to some of the more commonly used grid settings, such as turning grids or snap on and off.

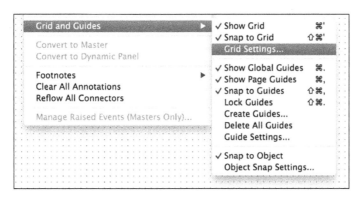

If we are looking for grid and layout templates for various mobile devices, the Axureland site and the Axure Forums are a good place to start if we don't want to create our own grid template from scratch.

Summary

So now we've gotten Axure 7 installed, registered, and taken a basic tour of the workspace and some of features we'll need to know more about when we start building our mobile prototypes. Axure 7 introduced some big changes in the way **Widget Styles and Properties** are managed (among many others that we will note in the following chapters). Widget libraries help us with existing components or to create new reusable components, making our prototyping more efficient. The consistent use of grids will give our designs a professional polish and make them appear much closer to the final app or website we want to build. We are now ready to start prototyping.

4
Building Mobile Prototypes

Now that we have Axure RP 7 installed and are familiar with the workspace, let's look at creating our first mobile prototype. There are several powerful features of Axure 7 we can take advantage of to create robust, highly interactive prototypes.

In this chapter we'll look at the following topics:

- Setting up a mobile prototype project
- Panel-centric designs
- Page-centric designs
- Managing displays with dynamic panels

Mobile prototypes

In previous versions of Axure, we used to start mobile projects by choosing the device where we wanted to use our prototype and designing for that screen resolution. But with Adaptive Views in Axure 7, that's all changed. We can now build a single Axure prototype with different views for smartphones, tablets, and desktop computers that are displayed based on the screen width of the device. We can also create landscape and portrait views for smartphones and tablets, allowing us to test or demonstrate how a responsive web design might appear to the final users.

Adaptive Views

Adaptive Views is one of the features of Axure 7 that is generating a lot of interest and attention. I'm going to hold off on a deeper dive into Adaptive Views until *Chapter 5, Adaptive Views*, while we walk through setting up a simple smartphone project so we can cover some of the basic Axure features while working with a one-screen view. We'll use this work later as a building block to explore Adaptive Views.

The first thing we'll want to do when creating the smartphone view of the prototype is decide which handheld device we'll be targeting for our work.

Targeting your device

Which device to target in mobile prototyping is a critical decision we have to make early in our project (before we even open Axure). Because Axure ultimately generates HTML and JavaScript files, and not native app code, we cannot assume that a prototype designed for one screen size will display correctly on other screen sizes. This is especially true of Android phones, which have a wide variety of possible screen sizes. It's essential that we know the device on which we will be testing or demonstrating the prototype and build to that screen resolution. This becomes extremely important if we conduct usability tests with the prototype because we are already placing the user in an unnatural situation if we are testing in a lab or just sitting beside them in a more natural setting asking them questions about what they are doing. Having a prototype that doesn't fit the screen correctly will further jeopardize the quality and reliability of our test results. I've seen poorly constructed prototypes ruin tests so try to avoid this mistake.

Looking at this small sample of screen resolutions for Apple, Android, and Microsoft devices, we can see there is variability in screen size even among a small set of smartphones and tablets. When you consider the vast diversity of Android devices, the number of screen resolutions increases exponentially.

Device	Screen resolution (pixels)
Samsung Galaxy S 3	720 x 1280
Samsung Galaxy S 4	1080 x 1920
Google Nexus 4	738 x 1280
Motorola Moto X	720 x 1280
iPhone 4S	640 x 960
iPhone 5	640 x 1136
iPad Mini	1024 x 768
iPad 2	1024 x 768
iPad with Retina	2048 x 1536
Windows Phone 7	480 x 800
Windows Phone 8	1280 x 768 (WXGA) and 1280 x 720p

 To learn more about screen density and pixel resolution, refer this article from *A List Apart* at http://alistapart.com/article/vexing-viewports.

For the purpose of our exercise, let's target the iPhone 5, which has a screen resolution of 640 x 1136 pixels. The concepts we'll cover apply to all mobile operating systems and their native apps, as well as the mobile internet. It's just the screen resolutions that will differ.

So let's create the initial view for our project.

Mobile screen setup

The first thing we'll do after creating a new project is use global guides to establish a screen canvas for us to work within. Since we have settled on using the iPhone 5 for our smartphone view, we will design our prototype at 320 x 568 pixels. We can create our prototype at half the pixel size of the actual iPhone 5 screen and set the width to device-width for the HTML viewport meta tag, which we control in the **Generate Prototype** dialog's **Mobile/Device** panel. Using the settings in the following screenshot, a prototype created at 320 x 568 will display correctly on the iPhone 5's higher resolution retina display as well as on non-Retina versions of the iPhone. Using the smaller size also makes the prototype files smaller and reduces the use of memory on the device, making the prototype download and run faster:

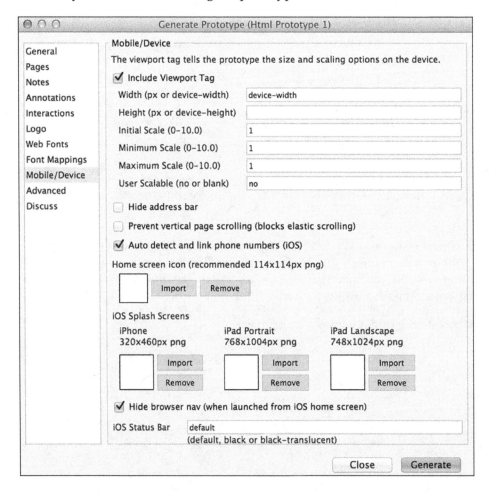

To learn more about the HTML viewport tag, refer to `https://developer.`
`mozilla.org/en-US/docs/Mozilla/Mobile/Viewport_meta_tag`.

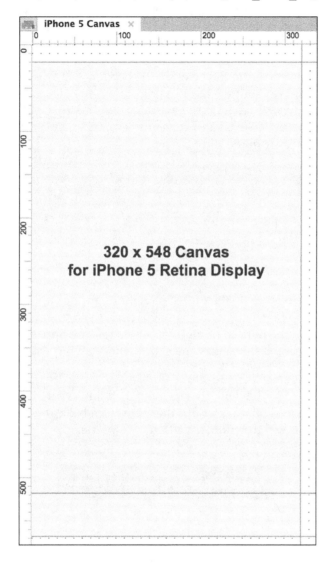

It's important to note that when creating guides in Axure there are two types, global guides and page guides. Global guides appear on every page of our prototype as it grows, while page guides only appear on the page where they were set. I prefer using global guides because while I like to make single-page panel-centric prototypes (discussed later), global guides are automatically on the page if you have to add a new one. Page guides are added to a page in Axure by dragging the mouse either down or to the right from the ruler on the border of the canvas. Global guides are added in the same way, but we have to hold down the *Command* key on Mac or the *Ctrl* key in Windows while dragging a guide from the top or left ruler. When we drag the guide down or across a page, a gray box will display its current pixel location so you can drop it in the right place:

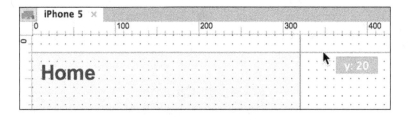

The next thing we'll do is create the global navigation for our app. Since we are simulating an iOS app for the iPhone 5, we will need to add a tab bar. The tab bar is the set of buttons at the bottom of many Phone apps and appears on most screens (unless we are designing full-screen games or media-viewing screens).

For our sample project, we'll create a four-button tab bar made up of four rectangles, measuring 80 x 50 pixels. This will give us a finished tab bar of 320 x 50 pixels. We can add graphics and labels later but this gives us a basic tab bar from which we set up the navigational functionality of our prototype:

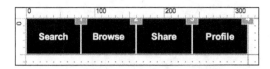

Pages and panels

The next decision we have to make (or really should have made already) is whether our app is going to be page-centric or panel-centric. In page-centric apps, each screen is created as its own page in Axure. In the panel-centric approach, we have one base page that holds the main navigation for a prototype and uses a Dynamic Panel to manage the views presented to a user. I prefer to use the panel-centric approach because it makes my prototypes more manageable. Panels are also needed to detect gestures, such as **OnSwipeLeft**, **OnSwipeRight**, **OnSwipeUp**, and **OnSwipeDown**, which are needed for building mobile interactions. The advantage of the panel-centric approach is that it allows us to download all the HTML and other code that Axure generates on the first page load, allowing subsequent screen changes to render faster and behave closer to the way a real mobile app does. The advantage of using a page-centric prototype is that it allows us to think of each screen as a discreet entity and is an easier way to think about Axure prototypes when we are first starting to work with mobile design. I use panel-centric designs because of fixed objects on the screens, such as headers and tab bars that I don't want to have to manage on each screen. I also like the faster response time as users explore the prototype. One thing to note when deciding which approach to take is that panel-centric prototypes don't have access to Axure's **OnPageLoad** event, except the first time the prototype is loaded (because it's all one HTML page). But the **OnPanelStateChange** event can be used to trigger interactions just as easily. Some prototypes require both approaches, meaning we can create most of the prototypes as panel-centric but still incorporate separate Axure pages for a full-screen display of functionality like a media player.

A panel-centric approach may cause a prototype to load more slowly because all the code is downloaded at once, but will also have a greater response time as users move from view to view because there are no more requests to the server. The panel-centric prototypes can also more easily take advantage of HTML5 caching on the device for online and offline use because there are fewer pages to include the manifest file.

A manifest file has to be created for every page that is going to be cached on the device using HTML5. For more information on creating a manifest file, refer to `http://westciv.com/tools/manifestR/`.

Once we create our tab bar, it's a good idea to group the widgets so we can move them around the screen as one unit. We'll want to position the tab bar unit beneath our content area (at x = 0, y = 518). In order to group widgets into one unit, select them all, right-click on them, and navigate to **Group** from the context menu.

Now that we've created our tab bar, we'll create a Dynamic Panel with multiple views for our content and add some touch targets to our tab bar so we can interact with our panels.

Dynamic Panels

Dynamic Panels are the defined regions of a screen that can have many of what Axure calls **States**. A simple example to think about is a module used to log in to a website. There could be a **Dynamic Panel** named **Login** with two states, or views, named **Login_Form** and **Login_Error**. We could then set **Login_Form** to display when the page is first shown to the user and show **Login_Error** only if the user doesn't enter their information correctly. Axure allows for some form validation to occur when buttons are tapped, so we can check the value the user typed in and determine what to do next. If the user enters their information correctly, we can have Axure direct them to another page.

Dynamic Panels, user inputs, and form field validation are some of the features that make Axure a powerful tool for creating highly interactive prototypes.

Now let's create a Dynamic Panel. The first thing we'll do is resize our content panel to be 320 x 518 pixels. It is now sitting above the tab bar, and not running underneath it. Then, we select it, right-click on it, and select **Convert to Dynamic Panel** from the context menu, as shown in the following screenshot:

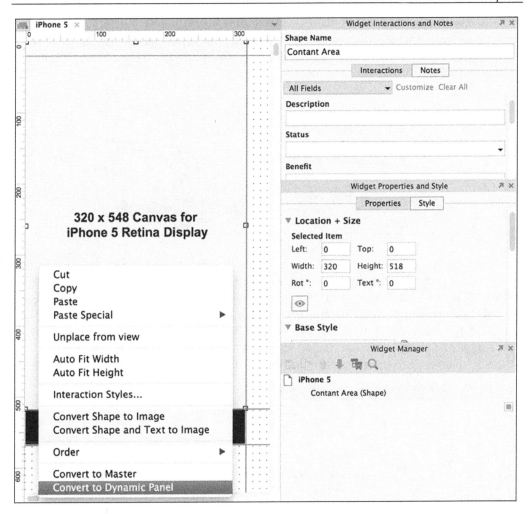

Once that's done, the widget named **Content Area** appears in the Dynamic Panel. As we can see in the **Widget Manager** panel, it has one default state named **State1**, which Axure automatically creates, and our **Content Area** rectangle is the content of that state. We can rename Dynamic Panels and states, and make any changes we want in the content.

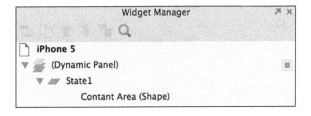

Now, we will rename our first state and create multiple states for each screen in our app. To rename a state, double-click on the name and type a new name. In order to add new states, right-click on a state and select **Add State** from the context menu, as shown in the following screenshot:

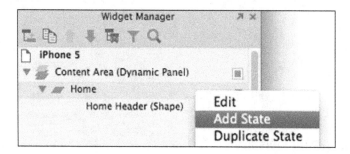

For our sample prototype, we will create five states, one to be reached by each button in the tab bar and an additional one for the home screen. When we create these states, we'll put a label widget in each one to mark the screen. We'll eventually delete the labels but they will provide an easy way for us to test our navigation before the screens have content. As we see in the **Widget Manager** panel, our prototype now has a dynamic panel with five named states (it's a best practice to always name states so that you can interact with them more easily when you use the **Case Editor**), as shown in the following screenshot:

Depending on the design of the app, the home screen may be a full-screen page that reveals child pages and the tab bar after the user takes some type of action, or the home screen may include the tab bar with either no tab selected or a home tab selected.

With this basic framework in place for our prototype, we are ready to start creating the navigation.

Navigation bars

Mobile apps frequently use navigation bars. For each operating system there is a convention for where navigation should be positioned on the screen (refer to the *Mobile operating system human interface guidelines* section in *Appendix, Axure and Mobile Design Resources*). On the iPhone, tab bars and tool bars are placed at the bottom of the screen. On Android and Windows devices, they can be placed at the top or bottom of the screen. Navigation placed at the bottom of the screen on Android phones can present a usability problem if a user accidently taps the hard or soft device buttons beneath the screen. You should come across this if you are usability testing your prototype with target users.

Interactivity

Using Axure's **OnClick** event, we will be able to create simple navigation to our four child screens. To add an event to our tab bar, select the individual widget that will have the event assigned to it. Events will now be listed in the **Interactions** screen of the **Widget Interactions and Notes** panel.

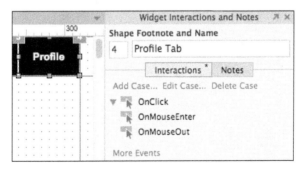

Events allow us to assign various behaviors to widgets in Axure. We can use them to display new screens, set variables, and interact with form elements that we have on the screen. In this example, we'll use the **OnClick** event to display one of the content states from our **Dynamic Panel**. Now let's take a look at the **Case Editor** and how we can use it create behaviors.

The Case Editor

The **Case Editor** is the part of Axure where we establish the behaviors that happen when events are triggered for any object. In our tab bar example, we will use the case editor to change the state of our **Content Area Dynamic Panel** when each of the four tabs is tapped.

 When prototyping for mobile in Axure, use the **OnClick** event for any interaction that will occur whenever the user taps an on-screen widget.

The **Case Editor** page is organized in three panels. The left-most one is the interaction we want to trigger. The center panel is used to organize the order in which we want multiple interactions to occur when there are more than one interactions. The right-most panel is where we will set the details of the interaction. In our example, we used the **Case Editor** to establish that when an **OnClick** event is detected by the widget named **Tab Four**, the Dynamic Panel named **Content Area** should display the **Screen Four** state, as shown in the following screenshot:

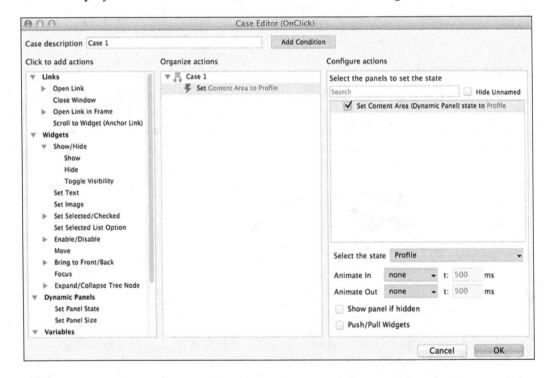

Once we do this with the other three tabs, we will have a basic iPhone 5 prototype with a tab bar that links to four screens. At this point, the basic project organization and navigation is complete. One last thing we could do is replace the rectangles in the tab bar with button images and create separate states for when they are selected. Prototyping to this level of detail will help us to better communicate the interactions and functionalities of our app. We'll have to decide on a case-by-case basis what degree of fidelity is needed for any given prototype.

The last thing we need to do, since this is an iPhone prototype, is anchor our tab bar to the bottom of the device window. This will allow content in the main viewing area to scroll underneath while always keeping our tab bar in the correct screen position for an iOS app.

To anchor a widget to the screen, convert it to a **Dynamic Panel** by selecting all the elements and choosing **Convert to Dynamic Panel** from the right-click context menu. Then click on the blue **None** link in the **Widget Properties and Style** dialog box, as shown in the following screenshot, to see the **Pin to Browser** dialog box.:

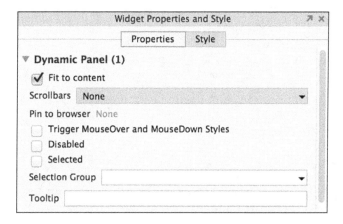

For an iPhone tab bar, which will sit as a fixed-position object on the screen, select the **Left** and **Bottom** options from the **Pin to Browser** dialog box, as shown in the following screenshot:

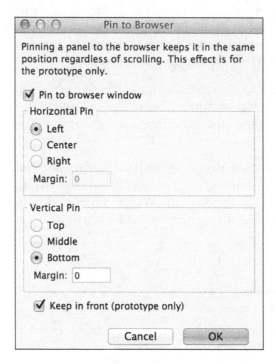

Summary

In this chapter, we looked at how to create a basic prototype for use on a mobile device. We created a **Dynamic Panel** to manage the various screens of the app, and created a basic tab bar as navigate to those screens. We also discussed panel-centric and page-centric prototypes. Now that we have a basic framework in place, we can start adding content and start thinking about how our content will be presented for different screen resolutions using Axure 7's new Adaptive Views functionality.

5
Adaptive Views

One of the most exciting features in Axure RP 7 is **Adaptive Views**. Adaptive Views is Axure's approach to simulating responsive web designs and prototyping for our complex multi-screen, multi-device world. Adaptive Views allow us to work on one page in an RP project, but create different views tailored to smartphones in landscape and portrait orientations, tablets in landscape and portrait orientations, and traditional desktop displays.

In this chapter, we'll look at:

- Creating and understanding the **Base View**
- Child page views and inheritance
- Designing for different device orientations
- Designing for phones and tablets

Planning Adaptive Views

Before we start creating our prototype, we need to decide what design approach we are going to use for a multi-device prototype. All the following three design approaches have their strengths and weaknesses (and should be thought through:

- **Mobile First**: In this approach, we design for the smallest screen first to make sure we provide the key functions and content of what we are designing to smartphone users and the constraints placed on them by smaller screens and unpredictable network connections. One of the key ideas behind Mobile First is that it forces us to decide what the really important functions are, and what we need to build for all users on all devices.

- **Desktop First**: In this approach, we design the desktop experience first so we can understand all the content that could be available and then design for progressively smaller screens. This allows us to have a 360 degree view of our digital experience before we start thinking about smaller screens and mobile contexts.

- **Tablet First**: In this approach, the tablet experience is designed first. This approach is appropriate when a majority of our site users are using tablets instead of desktops, laptops, or smartphones. Axure enables us to then design for larger and smaller screens and add, eliminate, or morph content accordingly.

The approach we take will depend on the project, what devices are most likely to be used with our design, and whether the project will be delivered in phases that give priority to one device over others. We may find that the correct approach is a hybrid of the three, so keep an open mind. In the sample Axure project we'll use in this chapter, we will take a Mobile First approach and focus on a fictitious mobile website so we can explore the features that support prototyping of responsive web designs. We'll use the iPhone 5 and iPad screen resolutions for example purposes, but Adaptive Views can be created to support any screen resolutions we want, including widescreen monitors and TVs.

I decided to use the iPhone and iPad as the target devices for this chapter because the screen-size ratios used in these devices are widely used in many mobile devices. The techniques described can be used on Android devices as well, many of which have amazing user experiences of their own. As mobile designers, we should be well versed in all platforms to better serve the people for whom we design.

Designing for Mobile First was a concept popularized by *Luke Wroblewski* in his book *Mobile First*.

Adaptive Views in Axure 7

In the previous versions of Axure, we used to start mobile projects by choosing the device where we wanted to use our prototype and designing for that screen resolution. But with Adaptive Views in Axure 7, that's all changed. We can now build a single Axure page with different views for smartphones, tablets, and desktop computers. And by using the shared projects feature in Axure, we can even allow different designers to work on different views for our application (although only one person can edit a page at a time, as in previous versions of Axure).

> For more information on shared projects, visit
> http://www.axure.com/features.

The Base View

The first thing we'll want to do is create a Base View for a page. A Base View in our Mobile First approach will be a handheld design, and from there we will work our way up to tablets. We should use a similar approach to responsive web design, in that we want to think through all the content elements for our views before we start our prototyping activities. This is where it's invaluable to sketch out the concepts for different screen sizes and get preliminary agreement from stakeholders before starting any serious work in Axure.

> When adding or removing content from our prototype, for example, changing a page heading, we should always consider doing so in the Base View because Axure's inheritance model will automatically make those updates to all the child views.

To create our Base View, we'll set up a page with page guides to mark out the screen real estate for our device. The examples in this chapter use the full screen width, but we need to be aware that the status bar and browser chrome of our target device also will occupy some of the screen. For our Base View, we'll design for when the phone is held in portrait orientation, the way people tend to hold their phones most of the time. We'll use page guides instead of global guides because the guides will change with each view.

The example in this chapter is a simple, fictitious, content-based site that features articles and tips about using Axure. We'll set up a page guide at 320 pixels to the right-hand side to mark the outer boundary of the device screen. We'll then add two more page guides at 10 pixels and 310 pixels to the right-hand side to create some margins to the left and right so our content is not bumping up against the edges of the screen (which may be obscured if the user has a case on their phone). Finally, we'll add a page guide at 568 pixels down to mark the bottom of the device screen. The page itself will include common elements such as a header, a footer, a featured article with image, and a list of other articles. These common elements should be created as a master, which will inherit all the views already in the project. If you create new views for a page already using an existing master, those are automatically added to the master.

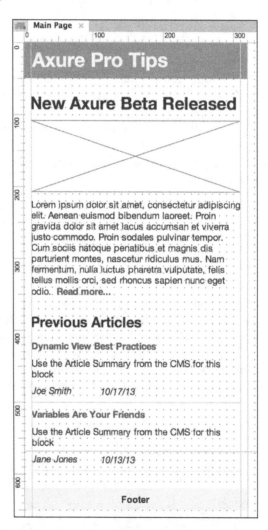

Now that we have created our Base View, we can start creating the variations that will take advantage of Adaptive Views' ability to detect changes in screen orientation. So let's move on to a landscape orientation design for a phone and see how Adaptive Views really works.

A different view

To create a new view, we click on the small blue icon (highlighted in red in the following screenshot) located to the left-hand side of the tab with the page name, which is **Main Page** in this example. This will bring up the Adaptive Views dialog.

The first time we open the Adaptive View dialog box, there will be no views in the list on the left-hand side (our Base View is not managed in this dialog). Clicking on the green + icon will enable the fields on the right-hand side where we create each view. In this example, we named the view `Phone Landscape`, set it to display when the screen is `321` pixels or wider, and set it to inherit from the base view. This setting and width is chosen because it means the screen will be wider than an iPhone in portrait orientation, which in our example means the phone must be tilted in a landscape orientation.

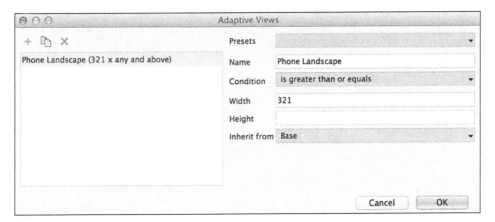

We can also use the built-in **Presets**, which allow us to quickly select from one of five popular device widths.

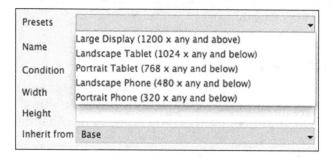

If we stopped with just this view, any device with a screen wider than 321 pixels would see the Phone Landscape view (even a desktop computer), but we will add more views to handle tablets after we finish the two phone views.

 Axure generates its prototypes as a mixture of HTML, JavaScript, and CSS code. The contents of any page are actually rendered in an HTML iframe. When we switch orientation, the device needs time to detect this and render the page again, showing the correct view. We may see slower response times as the screen reorients its display to the new orientation if we have a lot of other apps open on our device. In test sessions you want a device running just the mobile browser to improve the response time to orientation changes.

After we create our new view, the page tab changes and we see our Base View as well a new view Axure automatically labeled as **321** (the width we used as a breakpoint). The new view name is in an orange box because it is a child view of the **Base View**.

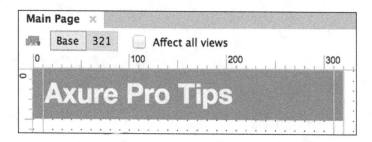

By clicking on the view name **321**, we make the iPhone landscape our active view for working. The active view is always displayed as a blue box. We can see that it starts out as an exact copy of the Base View from which it was created. Axure refers to this as **Inheritance** and it's an important concept that is new in Axure 7. Here is how Inheritance works:

- All the elements from the Base View are, by default, placed on the first new view that is derived from it.

- Any change made to an element in the Base View is inherited by all its children. We could rename our fictitious website in the header of the Base View and that change would propagate to all other views that are inherited from it.

- We can also create new views that inherit from views other than the Base View. This means that even if we create one base phone portrait view and have a second tablet view that is inherited from it, we can start designing a third desktop view that is inherited from the tablet view. The design implication of this is if we make changes to the tablet view (which won't affect its parent phone view) those changes will be reflected in the desktop view. This makes it easier for us to update the design for wider desktop screens using our tablet view as a starting point.

- Changes made in the child view don't affect the parent view, which is how we create specific views for phones in landscape orientation and tablets.

In addition to copying all the content from the Base View, Axure also adds a purple guide to show the breakpoint that triggers this view (in this case, **321** pixels from the left-hand side).

With our new **321** view in focus, we can begin designing how our website will look on a phone when it's held in landscape orientation and how we will simulate a responsive design.

In our iPhone landscape view, we can design the page to better fit within a 568 pixel wide iPhone screen (which will also scale to double that size on Retina devices). Any changes made here won't affect any design work in the Base View, and later we'll create another view to handle screen sizes wider than 568 pixels (for tablets). We can extend the header and footer, enlarge the photo to make better use of screen real estate, and increase the size of the headline. How we change elements in a child view is really up to the needs of our project, and could conceivably include an entirely different experience or greatly expanded functionality (as iOS 7 for iPhone does with its Calculator app). We also should add new page guides to this view to inform the width of our design and remind us where the bottom of the device is for a point of reference.

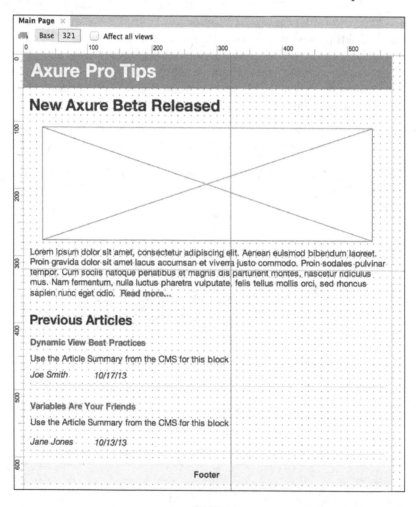

Expanding (or contracting) our designs

At this point we have covered the mechanics of creating a single Axure page that displays appropriately on an iPhone depending on device orientation. We can use these same techniques to design for tablets, laptops/desktops, and large format displays if we choose. We can also add content, such as a second column of articles and even an advertising unit as we scale up to tablets. The following example shows how we could approach the same design for our fictitious website when it's displayed on an iPad in portrait orientation. Again, all the content is inherited, which makes our work a little easier, but can also be altered as appropriate for the device.

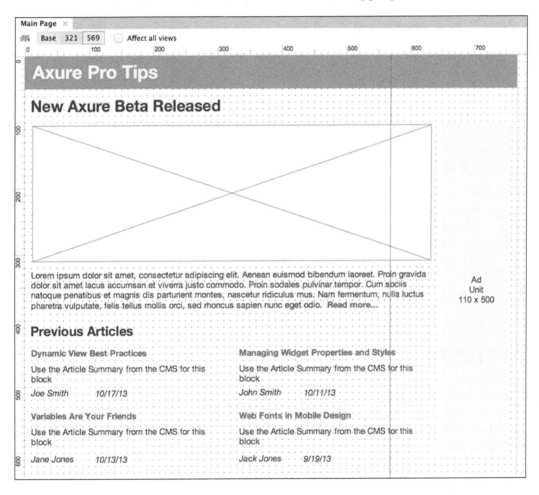

And in our project, we take it one step further by creating a view for the iPad in landscape orientation that includes one more column of content. This will leave us with a single Axure page that has four views depending on whether the device is a phone or tablet, and whether it is being held in landscape or portrait orientation. We finally have the ability to mimic the behavior of responsive web design without having to write any HTML or CSS.

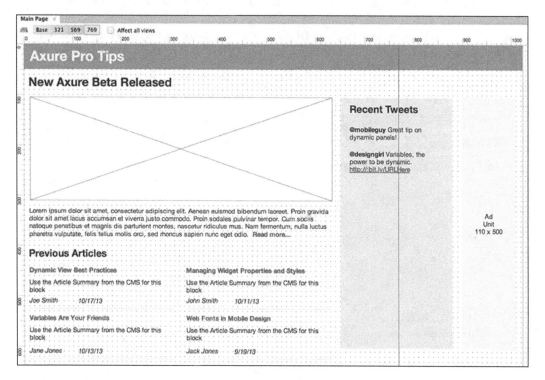

Summary

In this chapter we looked at Axure's new Adaptive Views feature. While it's not the same as writing responsive HTML and CSS with breakpoints, it does for the first time allow us to start prototyping for a responsive approach that recognizes our designs can be viewed on any device at any time; and we'd best be thinking about that from day one. We also saw that inheritance allows us to start a new view with all the content from a previous view as a base. This allows us to design more quickly and closely parallels how things work in a responsive web design. Now that we've looked at Adaptive Views, let's move into how we prototype some of the interactions that are unique to the mobile experience.

6
Mobile Interactions

Interactions and transitions are among the most critical and central (and really exciting) aspects of designing for mobile and touchscreen experiences. In the mobile space, we can explore interfaces where people have direct manipulation of the objects on the screen instead of working through intermediary devices, such as a mouse or keyboard. But this also introduces challenges for user experience designers, who have traditionally worked with tools, such as wireframes, that often represent a static state of a screen. While there are some designers doing great work documenting mobile interaction design in wireframes, nothing beats putting something "on the glass" and letting users and stakeholders interact with it using their own fingers on a real device. Fortunately, Axure started offering some features to support mobile design in Version 6.5, and Version 7 adds many new features for mobile designers.

In this chapter we'll look at:

- Gestures and Axure events that support them
- Off-canvas menus and layers
- Fixing elements to a single position on a screen
- Mobile-friendly forms
- Dialogs and alerts

Throughout the chapter, we'll be working with a prototype that simulates an iPhone native app to explore these topics. Our goal is to create a prototype similar to the following one, which is really a mostly empty shell of screens that simulates the menu interactions users may be familiar with from popular apps, such as Facebook, Gmail, and Path. At first glance, it looks like a simple prototype with two **Dynamic Panels**, but we'll see there is a lot going on beneath the surface.

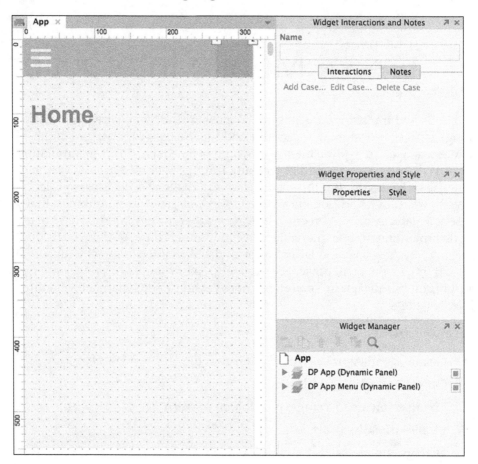

Gestures

Gestures are the main way people interact with mobile apps and websites. Users swipe in all directions, and they also tap, double-tap, and tap and hold. Other gestures that are available to people but are less commonly used are two to five finger multitouch, for example, pan, zoom in/out, and so on. Fortunately, some of these interactions are supported in Axure 7 and can be used to simulate fairly realistic experiences.

Swiping

Axure 7 supports swipe gestures through its event model. Four events available for smartphone and tablet design are **OnSwipeRight** and **OnSwipeLeft** from Axure 6.5, as well **OnSwipeUp** and **OnSwipeDown**, which were introduced in Axure 7. But these can only be used with **Dynamic Panels**, which is why I lean toward the panel-centric design approach outlined in *Chapter 4, Building Mobile Prototypes*. These four events are used to detect a person sliding their finger or thumb across a device's screen moving up, down, left, or right. In the following example, our sample app is one page, with several Dynamic Panels inside it to handle different screens. The main **Dynamic Panel** is named **DP App** and contains other panels for the app's header, content, and footer. **DP App** has been set up so that when a person swipes to the right another layer named **DP App Menu** is shown (advice about best practices for naming elements such as panels at `https://www.packtpub.com/sites/default/files/downloads/5145OT_Best_Practices.pdf`).

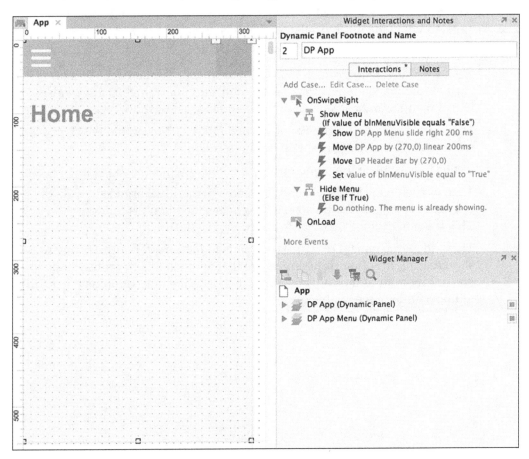

Using the OnLongClick event

Axure 7 adds a new gesture for mobile designers: **OnLongClick**. This event triggers cases and interactions just like the **OnClick** event, but is not triggered until the user taps an object and holds it for two seconds. In mobile interaction design, these actions are referred to as a **long press**.

 For examples of how a long press is used on Android, iOS, and Windows 8, refer to the *UX Booth* article on mobile interaction design by *Elaine McVicar* at http://www.uxbooth.com/articles/designing-for-mobile-part-2-interaction-design/.

Building a menu system

The actual mechanics of showing the menu is set up as a case named Show Menu that is triggered when the **OnSwipeRight** event is detected. Show Menu is set up as follows:

1. First, we navigate to **Project | Global Variables...** and create a global variable named blnMenuVisible. We will store the values **True** or **False** in this menu to indicate whether the menu is already showing.

2. Then we create a **Dynamic Panel** named **DP App Menu** that is 548 pixels tall by 270 pixels wide. This will hold our menu.

3. In this panel, create the menu options and link them to each page.

4. Then as each page loads, we check to see whether the variable blnMenuVisible is set to **False**, which means the menu is hidden. This is the trigger for this case to run.

5. Then, show the panel **DP App Menu** (it is hidden by default). The menu is shown using the **slide right** animation that is timed to 200 milliseconds to create a more fluid motion, and simulates it sliding onto the screen from the left-hand side of the visible canvas.

6. Move the panel **DP App** 270 pixels to the right-hand side using the **linear** animation, which simulates it being pushed off the right-hand side of the canvas by the menu.

7. Slide the panel **DP Header Bar** 270 pixels to the right-hand side using the **linear** animation. We have to move this panel separately because we used the **Pin to browser** option to fix it to the top of the screen (we'll look at this option in more detail later).

8. Set the blnMenuVisible variable to **True**. This will indicate to any other interface elements of the app that the menu is being shown (we'll look at some best practices for naming variables at https://www.packtpub.com/sites/default/files/downloads/5145OT_Best_Practices.pdf).

That may sound like a lot of actions to perform with one case, but they are actually quite easy to set up using the **Case Editor**.

Using conditions and actions

The first thing we do is use the **Condition Builder** to make sure our Show Menu case only runs when the menu is not visible.

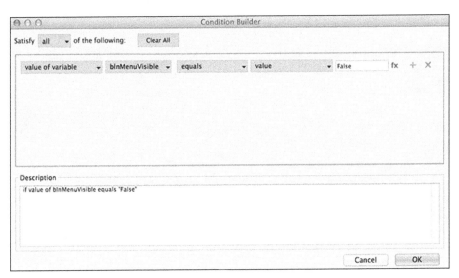

Once our condition trigger is set, we can use the **Case Editor** to chain the individual actions together to create a single user interaction. In the following example, we see in detail the first action we want to trigger, showing our menu. In the **Configure actions** column, for this action we select the **Dynamic Panel** we want to work with, and we select the **Show** option. We have also chosen the **slide right** animation type and set the time to 200 milliseconds.

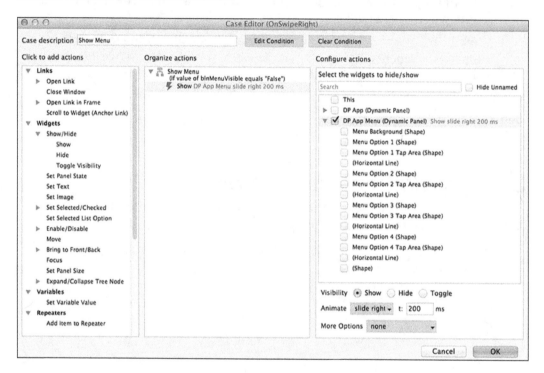

When using timing in events in mobile prototypes, there is a bit of fine-tuning needed as we switch from testing with a desktop browser to viewing the prototype on the device. This requires a bit of tweaking to longer or shorter times based on the processing power of the computer and device being used.

When we add all four actions to our **OnSwipeRight** event, the **Organize actions** column of the **Case Editor** will appear as in the following screenshot:

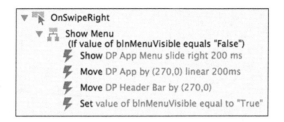

In the **Configure actions** panel for the second action, to move the **DP App** panel to the right, we set the panel to **Move** by 270 pixels to the right and also set it to use a **linear** animation timed to 200 milliseconds.

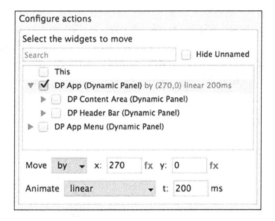

In the **Configure actions** panel for the third action, to move the **DP Header Bar** panel to the right, we set the panel to **Move** by 270 pixels to the right (along the x axis) and set it to use a **linear** animation timed to 200 milliseconds.

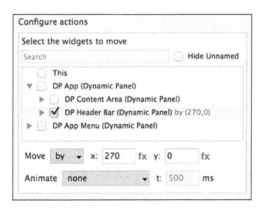

The final thing we do in **Configure actions** is to set our `blnMenuVisible` variable to **True** because the menu is now showing.

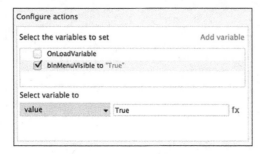

To hide the menu, we chain the same set of actions together but use **Hide** instead of **Show**. We also move the panel in the opposite direction by using negative values for the pixel distances and set the `blnMenuVisible` variable to **False**. Both interactions are shown in the **Widgets and Interaction Notes** panel for a tap area named **Header Menu Tap Area** that sits above our menu icon in **DP Header Bar**. For interface elements, such as buttons that people tap, we just attach our actions to the **OnClick** event instead of a gesture-triggered event, as seen in the following screenshot:

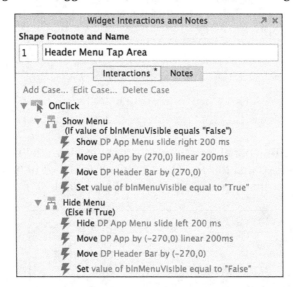

DP Header Bar and the highlighted tap area are shown in the following screenshot:

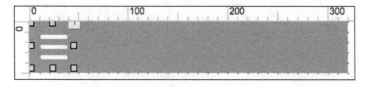

And the menu we just built appears in the following screenshot:

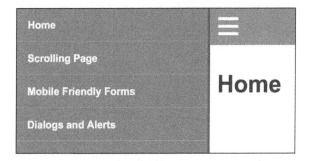

We have now built a framework for a reusable menu system that mimics some common behaviors seen in many mobile apps. We have connected our user interactions to both taps and gestures, and seen how several actions can be chained together to create a realistic mobile experience. Now, let's look at how we deal with one of the realities of mobile design: delays in screen refreshes.

A loader

Delays in screen refreshing are a common occurrence in mobile apps and websites. They are an inherent by-product of unpredictable and sometime unavailable network connections, the amount of data being downloaded, and general app stability. A common UI pattern has emerged, which is to display an animation to signify something is indeed happening after a user does something and provide feedback to the user that they have to wait. These animations can take one of several forms, including text that reads **Loading…** in which the ellipses are animated to cycle through the three periods. Another common pattern is a circle with an animated set of lines that continually move around the circle (a loader or spinner in mobile design terms) until the next screen displays. Let's look at an easy way to create a loader in our mobile prototypes.

The graphic

The first thing we need is an animated GIF file. There are many available in free Axure widget libraries and from other sources. You can also generate and download one online at the *ajaxload.info* web page (`http://www.ajaxload.info`), which is what we'll use in this example.

The interaction

The setup for our RP file is simple. We create a **Dynamic Panel** named **DP Contents** with three states. The **Screen One** state is the first screen the user sees. The **Loader** state holds the animated GIF file. The **Screen Two** state is the screen the user is directed to after a timed display of the **Loader** state.

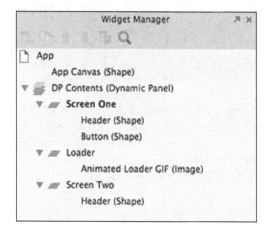

The next thing to do is create an **OnClick** event on the button in the **Screen One** panel. That event should trigger three actions:

- Set the panel state to **Loader**
- Wait for 1000 milliseconds
- Set the panel state to **Screen Two**

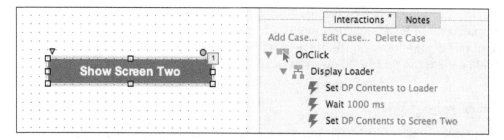

Our loader is now complete. If we want to test how people react to slower or faster responses from our app, we just have to adjust the time. While faster interactions seem like they'd be better, there will be cases where a slightly slower animation does a better job of communicating what is happening and can create a richer user experience. This is why we iterate and test with prototypes.

Dialogs and Alerts

Another common interaction seen in mobile websites and apps are pop-up alerts or notifications. Reproducing these in Axure 7 is easy and just involves working with a **Dynamic Panel**. In the following example, we'll work with a pop-up panel that has two states, one for when the user does not select a required checkbox and one for when they do but we want to confirm the selection. The logic that determines which state is displayed is tied to the **OnClick** event of the **I Accept** button.

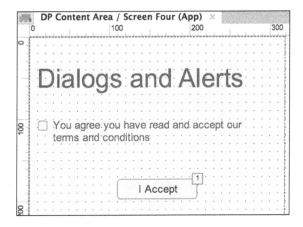

We've already covered how Dynamic Panels are created and managed, but let's look at the logic we create in the **Case Editor** for our dialog. Our Dynamic Panel, **DP Alert**, has two states: one for when the user doesn't select the checkbox and one to confirm their selection when they do. This is all we need to do to trigger the display of either layer based on what the user does.

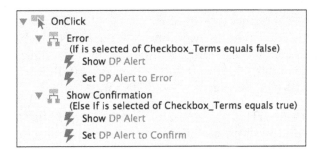

In the following screenshot, we see one of the panel states, in this case the one triggered when the user has selected the checkbox. And with this, our look at pop-ups and dialogs is complete.

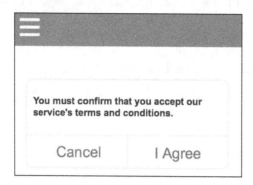

Mobile forms

One of the many new features in Axure 7 that specifically targets mobile design is support for mobile-friendly form field types, which can trigger the display of a context-specific keyboard. That is, when a user needs to enter an e-mail address, they are given a keyboard with all the necessary characters. We discussed this topic briefly in *Chapter 2, Mobile Design Concepts*, but we'll look at it in a little more detail now.

These new form field types were introduced as part of HTML5 and replace the familiar `<input type="text" />` tag with additional inputs for e-mail addresses, URLs, numeric values, and phone numbers. The results of using these on a mobile website is that when a user taps into a form field, the keyboard they are presented with includes all the characters they need for that field type instead of the default QWERTY keyboard. This saves the user time flipping between keyboards to enter characters, such as a colon, backslash, @ symbol, or digits. In the case of `<input type="tel" />`, the mobile browser displays the same 10-digit keypad used to make calls, with its nice big buttons and no text characters.

Because Axure generates HTML pages in the final prototype, these fields can be used in our projects whether we are simulating a mobile website or a native app.

Form field attributes are set in the **Widget Properties and Style** panel. The field type is chosen from the **Type** select menu. The **Hint Text** field populates the placeholder attribute of the form field. In the following e-mail field example, someone writing HTML would write it as `<input type="email" placeholder="Email Address" />`.

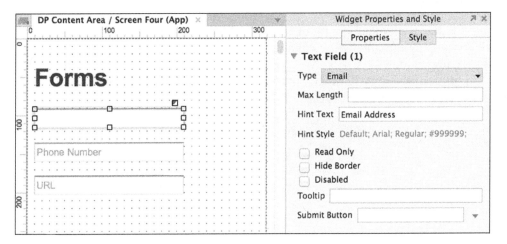

When the user taps into the field, the placeholder text is removed and the user can type their own information with an appropriate keyboard, as seen in the following screenshot from iOS 7 on an iPhone:

Now that we've seen how form interactions have been improved in Axure 7, let's look at our final topic for this chapter, drag-and-drop events.

Summary

In this chapter we looked at a lot of topics. We built a menu system that supports navigation using tap and swipe gestures. We saw how dialogs and alerts can be created using Dynamic Panels. And we saw how Axure 7 makes form fields easier to work with in a mobile context. Now that we've seen how some basic mobile interactions can be created in Axure 7, let's look at drag-and-drop events.

7
Drag-and-drop

One of the most common mobile interactions is dragging and dropping objects on the device screen. While this interaction is commonly used in mobile gaming, it's also seen in popular apps such as Facebook, which uses drag interactions to dismiss chat heads (icons representing private messages between Facebook friends) from the screen. In this chapter we'll look at:

- Drag-and-drop interactions
- Axure 7 drag events

Using OnDrag and OnDragDrop events

In the following example we'll use the **OnDrag** and **OnDragDrop** events of Axure to simulate a similar interaction in a prototype. To illustrate this chapter, we're going to take the same RP file we created in *Chapter 6, Mobile Interactions*, and add a screen to show drag-and-drop. The example we are going to build mimics the functionality of Facebook's chat heads feature. In the following screenshot, we can see the final outcome in which the image at the bottom of the screen (the circle labeled with the X) was moved onto the screen once a user started dragging the circle labeled with a Y.

The first thing we'll need to do is create two circular widgets. I refer to them as the drag object and the drag target. The drag object is the element that users will manipulate, while the drag target is the object we want users to move the drag object over to trigger our interaction. You can turn a rectangle widget into a circle by editing its settings in the **Widget Properties and Style** panel. The finished objects are shown in the following screenshot:

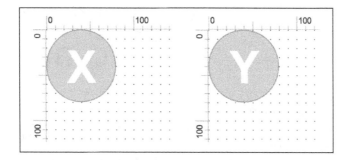

We then need to convert each of the circles we created into **Dynamic Panels** because the two drag events we will use are only triggered on **Dynamic Panels**. First select the circle widget named **X**, right-click on it, choose **Convert to Dynamic Panel** from the context menu, and name the panel DP Drag Object. Then select the circle widget named **Y**, right-click on it, choose **Convert to Dynamic Panel** from the context menu, and name this panel DP Drag Target. We now have the two objects that will be used in our drag-and-drop interaction. **DP Drag Object** is the widget we will drag on the screen with our finger and **DP Drag Target** is the object we are going to try and drag it toward.

In the example for this chapter, **DP Drag Object** is positioned at coordinates (230, 100). **DP Drag Target** is positioned at coordinates (120, 600). This positions **DP Drag Object** near the right-hand side of the screen and 100 pixels from the top. **DP Drag Target** is positioned off the screen, but will move onto the screen when we start to drag **DP Drag Object** with our finger.

Our interaction will be triggered solely based on what the user does with **DP Drag Object**. We will attach two actions to the **OnDrag** event for that **Dynamic Panel**, one to allow **DP Drag Object** to be dragged and another to move **DP Drag Target** onto the screen and position it at coordinates (120, 300).

To do this, double click on the **OnDrag** event for **DP Drag Object**. This will bring up the **Case Editor**. First add a **Move** action from the **Click to add actions** column and then select the **with drag** option with no animation from the **Configure actions** column. Both selections are highlighted with red boxes in the following example. With these two actions, **DP Drag Object** is now draggable.

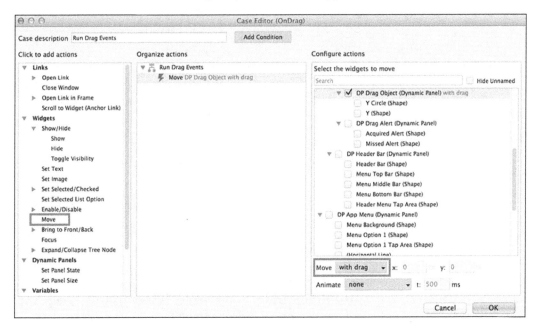

In the second action, we use **Move** again, this time to bring the **DP Drag Target** panel from off the canvas to a position at the bottom of the screen. To do this, add a second **Move** action in the **Case Editor**. Move **DP Drag Target** to coordinates (120, 300). Select a linear animation timed for 200 milliseconds. Both selections are highlighted with red boxes in the following example.We now have one draggable UI element that when moved causes a second UI element to slide up onto the screen.

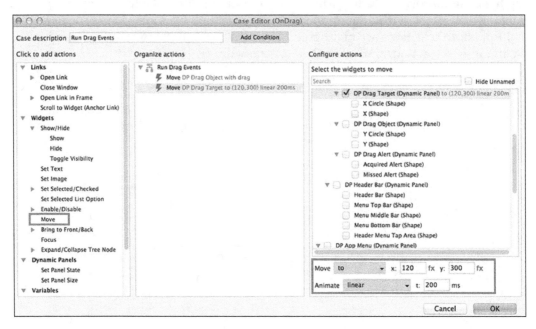

We now need to set up the draggable object and the target to complete our interaction. To do that, we'll use the **OnDragDrop** event of Axure. The **OnDragDrop** event is triggered when a user stops moving a draggable object across the screen. In our example, we test for one of two conditions, which we set up using the **Case Editor**. In our example we check for whether or not **DP Drag Object** is over the **DP Drag Target**, and then run a set of actions based on the result. If **DP Drag Object** is over **DP Drag Target**, we'll display a confirmation message that is in **Dynamic Panel DP Drag Alert**. If **DP Drag Object** is not over **DP Drag Target**, we'll display another message using the same **Dynamic Panel**.

The **OnDragDrop** event is also set up to hide the drag target and slide the drag object off screen when they overlap, completing our simulation of how this interaction can work. What we do with our own animations and transitions is really up to us and the effect we are trying to create. We can see the **OnDrag** and **OnDragDrop** events in the following screenshot. They are created in the Case Editor like the other examples in this chapter.

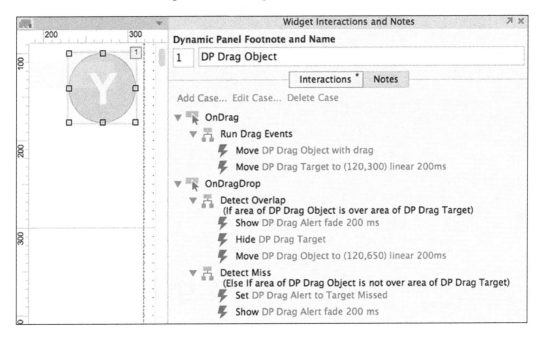

Summary

In this chapter we saw a sample of what can be done with Axure 7 drag-and-drop events. Now that we've covered the basics of mobile prototyping in Axure, let's look at how we get our prototypes on a real device for demonstration and testing.

8
Viewing on Mobile Devices

The main reason for creating a prototype is to exercise a design idea to see if it matches the expectations of stakeholders and can be easily used by the people for whom we are designing. If it doesn't, and we fail, that's OK. That's why we make prototypes. Failing fast and learning from that are important parts of iterative design.

Axure 7 makes it easy to get our work on real devices so we can test out ideas on a device in the lab or field, and so we can let stakeholders experience the design on the intended device with their own hands.

In this chapter we'll look at:

- Publishing prototypes to AxShare
- Creating home screen icons
- Creating app splash pages
- Publishing to Dropbox or internal web servers
- Creating QR codes to access prototypes

Hosting prototypes

To let users access our prototype on their own devices or the one we control for demonstration or usability testing, we are going to need to find a way to host it in an available web server. Fortunately, because our prototype is a collection of web pages and related files, we can use any web server that can be accessed by the device in question.

AxShare

One of the easiest ways to get our prototype on a device and in the hands of users is to use the free AxShare service as a hosting environment. To publish to AxShare, you first need to set up an AxShare account. To do this, go to `http://share.axure.com` and you'll be able to create a free account that allows for the hosting of 10 prototypes. If you need to host more prototypes or want a custom domain, there is also an AxShare subscription product. Once the account is created, publishing a prototype to AxShare just requires a click on the **AxShare** button in the top toolbar pane of the prototype editor.

When we publish to AxShare, we see the dialog box as shown in the following screenshot. We use it to sign in to our AxShare account and can save the sign in credentials. In this dialog box, we can choose to create and upload a new prototype or update an existing one, and decide if we want to use password protection to restrict access to our work. When a new prototype is uploaded to AxShare, it will automatically create a prototype ID that allows people to access it using a mobile web browser.

Remember that Axure ultimately creates HTML files, even when we are simulating full-screen native apps. We'll see the dialog box shown in the following screenshot when publishing, which confirms we are uploading our files and provides us with the URL we can use to get the prototype on a mobile browser. The random characters at the end of the URL are the prototype ID that AxShare created.

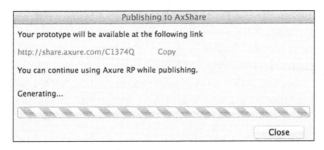

One thing to note is that the URL provided in the dialog box links to the main prototype page, which includes the left panel used to navigate pages or do variable debugging. When sending a prototype to a mobile device, we are going to want to get the exact URL of our home screen and not the main prototype file. This means the URL for a prototype at `http://share.axure.com/C1374Q/` will need to be updated to include a specific screen URL so it ends up being more like `http://share.axure.com/C1374Q/publishing.html`. We can get this URL by closing the left navigation panel after selecting our start screen, and then copying the URL from the desktop browser address bar. And with this URL the person accessing it on a phone is getting our intended start page.

One thing to be aware of when hosting prototypes on AxShare or any cloud-based solution is that there may be network latency just as there is with real mobile websites due to the speed of the network being used and general network traffic. If we need the prototype to behave more real like a native app in which much of the user interface and some data is already on the device, we should consider using HTML 5 device caching as discussed in *Chapter 4, Building Mobile Prototypes*.

Home screen icons and splash pages

If we want our app to look like it is running in full-screen mode like a native app, we can add a home screen icon, an iOS splash screen, and hide the browser's navigation. To do this, add the home screen and splash page PNG images at the sizes specified in the **Mobile/Device** panel of the **Generate Prototype** dialog box. We also need to select the checkboxes for the **Hide address bar** and **Hide browser nav (when launched from iOS home screen)** options. This panel is also used to generate the HTML viewport meta tag and instruct the mobile browser to hide the address bar and browser navigation in iOS. We can also set the iOS status bar to use the default appearance, a black background, or a black translucent background. For each prototype, we'll want to experiment with these settings to see which works best for our project.

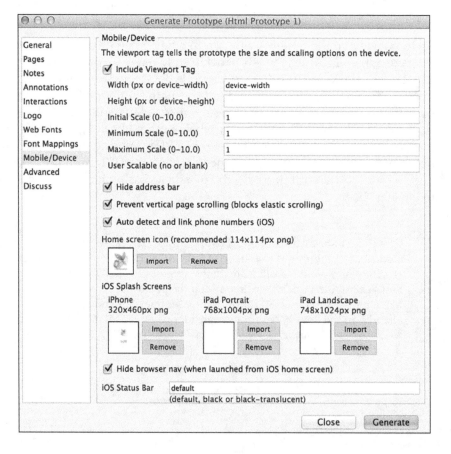

We can add the prototype to the home screen using native browser and OS functionality (this differs between iOS and Android, and even between different versions of Android). On an iPhone 5 which is running on iOS 7, our PNG image appears as an iPhone home screen as shown in the following screenshot:

The splash screen will load as a full-screen image prior to our main prototype page loading, so users see a full-screen image as seen in the following screenshot, when they first tap the home screen icon to open our prototype. This is one way to make our prototype feel more like a native app.

Dropbox and internal servers

Another option for hosting our prototype is to use a free service, such as Dropbox or an internal web server. We may have to use an internal web server if we are testing with devices that are behind a corporate firewall.

If we are hosting on Dropbox, just use the Mac Finder or Windows Explorer to locate the page for which you need a URL. Select the HTML file, right-click on it, and select **Copy Public Link** from the content menu. We have now captured a URL that we can share with other devices in an e-mail, text message, or embedded in a QR code.

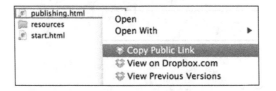

We sometimes have to host our prototypes on internal servers to protect proprietary designs. When we do this, we'll need to provide mobile devices for usability test participants and possibly for internal stakeholders if their devices cannot connect to the internal network where our prototype is hosted.

Loading the prototype to a real device

Once we have a URL we want to direct users to, there are several ways to get it on their device. URLs can be sent via e-mail, text message, or scanned to a device using a QR code. **Kaywa** offers a great free service for generating QR codes. This option lets us print the QR code so each test or demo participant can scan it with a QR reader such as Red Label as they enter the lab or demo session. Kaywa provides a few different options we will want to explore. You can learn more at the Kaywa website at http://qrcode.kaywa.com.

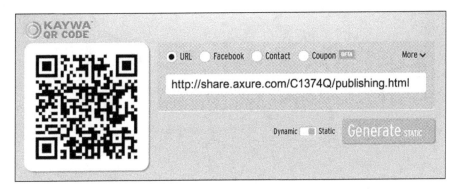

Summary

In this chapter we saw how prototypes can be tested or demonstrated on mobile devices using tools, such as AxShare, Dropbox, or an internal web server. We also saw how we can get that URL to our target devices, using methods such as e-mail, text messages, or a scanned QR code. We have now covered how to build a mobile prototype and how to get it on a device for testing or demonstration. With the knowledge we now have, let's start making awesome things.

Axure and Mobile Design Resources

Online resources

One of the great aspects of working with Axure and mobile design is that there are a lot of free resources online. Mobile operating system creators publish their own design guidelines. Many thoughtful writers have published great articles and blog posts, the product team at Axure provides a wealth of examples, and many people are creating sharing widget libraries or functional RP files within the Axure community. These are just few of the many resources available, but the ones I visit the most are as follows:

Resources from Axure

You can visit the Axure forums at `http://www.axure.com/forum`

You can visit the Axure training videos and tutorials at `http://www.axure.com/learn`

Widget libraries

You can visit the Axutopia widget libraries at `http://axutopia.com`

You can visit the widget libraries from Axure and the user community at `http://www.axure.com/download-widget-libraries`

You can visit the Totalwireframe widget libraries at `http://totalwireframe.com`

You can visit the jQuery Mobile Axure widgets at `http://axureland.com/axure_widget_libraries/entry/jquery_mobile_widgets`

General Axure and mobile design resources

You can visit the Axureland blog, tutorials, and widget libraries at `http://www.axureland.com`

You can visit *Best Practices in Axure* by *Jeff Yam* at `http://jeffyam.com/node/201`

You can visit the *Advanced Mobile Prototyping* by *Luca Benazzi* at `http://www.humaneinterface.net/advanced-mobile-prototyping-in-axure-rp-pro-tips-and-examples/`

You can visit the AxureWorld online event and tutorials at `http://www.axureworld.org/`

You can refer to *Touch Gesture Reference Guide* by *Luke Wroblewski* at `http://www.lukew.com/touch`

You can visit the mobile design articles of *Smashing Magazine* at `http://mobile.smashingmagazine.com/`

You can download the teehan+lax iPhone Photoshop file at `http://www.teehanlax.com/tools/iphone/`

You can download the teehan+lax iPad Photoshop file at `http://www.teehanlax.com/tools/ipad/`

You can refer to *Dive Into HTML 5* by *Mark Pilgrim* at `http://diveintohtml5.info/`

You can refer to *Responsive Resources* by *Brad Frost* at `http://bradfrost.github.io/this-is-responsive/resources.html`

Technical documentation

You can visit the Axure release history at `http://www.axure.com/release-history`

You can visit the Axure API at `http://www.axure.com/axure-rp-api`

Human interface guidelines for mobile operating systems

For iOS, visit `https://developer.apple.com/library/ios/documentation/UserExperience/Conceptual/MobileHIG/Introduction/Introduction.html`

For Android, visit `http://developer.android.com/design/index.html`

For Microsoft Windows phone, visit `http://developer.windowsphone.com/en-us/design`

For BlackBerry, visit `http://developer.blackberry.com/native/documentation/cascades/ui/index.html`

Index

Symbols

Thank you for buying
Mobile Prototyping with Axure 7

About Packt Publishing

Packt, pronounced 'packed', published its first book "*Mastering phpMyAdmin for Effective MySQL Management*" in April 2004 and subsequently continued to specialize in publishing highly focused books on specific technologies and solutions.

Our books and publications share the experiences of your fellow IT professionals in adapting and customizing today's systems, applications, and frameworks. Our solution based books give you the knowledge and power to customize the software and technologies you're using to get the job done. Packt books are more specific and less general than the IT books you have seen in the past. Our unique business model allows us to bring you more focused information, giving you more of what you need to know, and less of what you don't.

Packt is a modern, yet unique publishing company, which focuses on producing quality, cutting-edge books for communities of developers, administrators, and newbies alike. For more information, please visit our website: www.packtpub.com.

Writing for Packt

We welcome all inquiries from people who are interested in authoring. Book proposals should be sent to author@packtpub.com. If your book idea is still at an early stage and you would like to discuss it first before writing a formal book proposal, contact us; one of our commissioning editors will get in touch with you.

We're not just looking for published authors; if you have strong technical skills but no writing experience, our experienced editors can help you develop a writing career, or simply get some additional reward for your expertise.

Instant Axure RP Starter

ISBN: 978-1-84969-516-9   Paperback: 70 pages

Start prototyping your first Axure RP project the
easy way

1. Learn something new in an Instant!
   A short, fast, focused guide delivering
   immediate results

2. Helping you learn the fundamentals of Axure
   RP, while making prototypes

3. Focus on only the most important features,
   saving you time and helping you to start using
   Axure RP immediately

Axure RP 6 Prototyping Essentials

ISBN: 978-1-84969-164-2   Paperback: 446 pages

Creating highly compelling, interactive prototypes
with Axure that will impress and excite decision
makers

1. Quickly simulate complex interactions for
   a wide range of applications without any
   programming knowledge

2. Acquire timesaving methods for constructing
   and annotating wireframes, interactive
   prototypes, and UX specifications

3. A hands-on guide that walks you through the
   iterative process of UX prototyping with Axure

Creating Mobile Apps with jQuery Mobile

ISBN: 978-1-78216-006-9   Paperback: 254 pages

Learn to make practical, unique, real-world sites that span a variety of industries and technologies with the world's most popular mobile development library

1. Write less, do more: learn to apply the jQuery motto to quickly craft creative sites that work on any smartphone and even not-so-smart phones

2. Learn to leverage HTML5 audio and video, geolocation, Twitter, Flickr, blogs, Reddit, Google maps, content management system, and much more

3. All examples are either in use in the real world or were used as examples to win business across several industries

Developing Mobile Games with Moai SDK

ISBN: 978-1-78216-506-4   Paperback: 136 pages

Learn the basics of Moai SDK through developing games

1. Develop games for multiple platforms with a single code base

2. Understand the basics of Moai SDK

3. Build two prototype games including one with physics

4. Deploy your game to iPhone'

Please check **www.PacktPub.com** for information on our titles

www.ingramcontent.com/pod-product-compliance
Lightning Source LLC
LaVergne TN
LVHW080100070326

832902LV00014B/2341